Fortress • 20

British Home Defences 1940–45

Bernard Lowry • Illustrated by Chris Taylor & Vincent Boulanger

Series editors Marcus Cowper and Nikolai Bogdanovic

First published in Great Britain in 2003 by Osprey Publishing,
Midland House, West Way, Botley, Oxford OX2 0PH, UK
443 Park Avenue South, New York, NY 10016, USA
Email: info@ospreypublishing.com
© 2004 Osprey Publishing Ltd.

ISBN 978 1 84176 767 3

Editorial: Ilios Publishing, Oxford, UK (www.iliospublishing.com)
Maps by The Map Studio,
Index by Alison Worthington
Design: Ken Vail Graphic Design, Cambridge, UK
Originated by PPS Grasmere Ltd., Leeds, UK
Printed in China through Bookbuilders

07 08   10 9 8 7 6 5 4 3 2

A CIP catalogue record for this book is available from the British Library.

FOR A CATALOGUE OF ALL BOOKS PUBLISHED BY OSPREY MILITARY AND AVIATION
PLEASE CONTACT:

NORTH AMERICA
Osprey Direct, C/o Random House Distribution Center, 400 Hahn Road,
Westminster, MD 21157
E-mail: info@ospreydirect.com

ALL OTHER REGIONS
Osprey Direct UK, P.O. Box 140, Wellingborough, Northants, NN8 2FA, UK
E-mail: info@ospreydirect.co.uk

www.ospreypublishing.com

Author's note

Many people have helped me in writing this book. I would firstly
like to thank my wife, Geraldine, who helped me in countless ways.
Mick Wilks provided not only inspiration during long periods in the
National Archives, Kew, but also unstinting advice and the generous
provision of material for this book. I am also grateful to Dr Mike
Osborne, John Guy, Colin Jones and the Roden family for their help
too. The staff at the National Archives and Imperial War Museum
should also be mentioned, as should Nikolai and Marcus at Ilios
Publishing. If this book has a dedication, it is to the people of these
islands who, whilst not directly engaged in the conflict, were still
very much 'doing their bit'.

Readers who would like to learn more about 20th-century
fortifications may wish to consult the following websites:
Site O
    www.siteo.net
The Pillbox Study Group
    www.pillbox-study-group.org.uk

Image credits

The following abbreviations appear in the photographic credits in
this work. Unless otherwise indicated, the images are from the
author's collection.

BPC	Bamforth Postcard Collection
CET	Coventry Evening Telegraph
EH	English Heritage/National Monuments Record collection
IWM	Imperial War Museum, London, photographic archive (with image reference number)
IT	Imperial Tobacco
MO	Dr Mike Osborne
MW	Mick Wilks Collection
NA	National Archives, Kew, UK image library (with image reference number)
NJCP	Nigel J. Clarke Publications, (www.njcpublications.demon.co.uk)
PB	Penguin Books Ltd.
RF	The Roden family
SB	Sam Beard

Linear measurements

Distances, ranges, and dimensions are given in Imperial values in
this volume:

1 inch (in.)	2.54 cm	1 mile	1.609 km
1 foot (ft)	0.3048 m	1 pound (lb)	0.4536 kg
1 yard (yd)	0.9144 m		

The Fortress Study Group (FSG)

The object of the FSG is to advance the education of the public
in the study of all aspects of fortifications and their armaments,
especially works constructed to mount or resist artillery. The FSG
holds an annual conference in September over a long weekend
with visits and evening lectures, an annual tour abroad lasting
about eight days, and an annual Members' Day.

The FSG journal *FORT* is published annually, and its newsletter
Casemate is published three times a year. Membership is
international. For further details, please contact:
The Secretary, c/o 6 Lanark Place, London W9 1BS, UK

Contents

Introduction

We shall defend our island, whatever the cost may be. We shall fight on the beaches, we shall fight on the landing grounds, we shall fight in the fields and in the streets, we shall fight in the hills. We shall never surrender.
Winston Churchill, in a speech to the House of Commons, 4 June 1940

Britain, by virtue of her island position, had escaped the wars that had swept across continental Europe in the 18th and 19th centuries. A powerful navy had ensured that the surrounding seas were safe. World War I had seen an aggressive Germany approaching closer to the British Isles, and anti-invasion defences were erected in the east and south-east of England. As long as Germany was locked into static warfare on the Western Front the greatest threat to the island's population came from aerial attacks by German airships, Gotha and AEG bombers, and from the shelling of east-coast towns by the German fleet. The threat diminshed at war's end, but in the inter-war years the rise of Nazism and the re-arming of Germany posed a new threat. At the end of the 1930s the British Army, after years of budgetary neglect, was in a woeful condition, quite unfit to fight a modern war, being short of modern equipment and lacking sufficient training. In addition, UK forces had imperial responsibilities to attend to.

The fear of an aerial bombing campaign and of a fatal, 'knockout blow' meant that protecting Britain from air attack was given priority: a radar early-warning chain was put in place. This arrived in time for the outbreak of World War II and stations were placed along the south and east coasts: this, plus a rapidly expanding fighter force, would prove invaluable in the Battle of Britain.

The lightning campaign unleashed by Germany against Poland on 1 September 1939 ushered in World War II. On 3 September Britain and France declared war on Germany, the conscription of men up to the age of 41 was introduced, a strict blackout was imposed, and on the following day the British Expeditionary Force (BEF) was sent to France. Apart from the dropping of leaflets by the Royal Air Force on German cities, there was a reluctance by the Allies to do more than make plans and await Germany's next move: so began the 'Phoney War'.

On the seas, however, war began early with the sinking of the *Royal Oak* by *U-47* in Scapa Flow on 14 October, together with bombing attacks on coastal shipping. A week later, Winston Churchill, then First Sea Lord was moved to write to the Chiefs of Staff posing the question: what would happen if 20,000 enemy troops were to land on the east coast of England?

In November the first bombs fell on British soil. German reconnaissance aircraft flew over Britain taking aerial photographs of possible targets, a process begun before World War II by the German national airline Lufthansa on its scheduled flights to the UK. A hard winter delayed the German attack in the west and it was said by the British premier, Neville Chamberlain, that Hitler had 'missed the bus'. The BEF, in their sector of northern France, waited, trained and started to build defensive positions along the Belgian border: these included reinforced concrete pillboxes for machine and anti-tank (AT) guns, AT ditches, as well as trench works reminiscent of World War I, for both Britain and France were expecting a re-run of that war.

After the winter lull, fighting resumed again in April 1940 when Germany invaded Denmark and Norway. Whilst the capture of Denmark was relatively bloodless, the fighting for Norway was in earnest. The French and British force was defeated, as much as anything through their own indecision, delay and lack of supplies, although Germany suffered significant losses, especially of aircraft and warships. Nevertheless, Germany was now about to close the noose about France and the Low Countries.

Unlike the Germans, who operated as a unified whole, the Allies faced many organisational difficulties. In the early-1930s, assured that Belgium was her ally, France had embarked upon a series of colossal fortifications along her borders with Germany and fascist Italy, named after the then Minister of War, André Maginot (see Fortress 10: *The Maginot Line 1928–45*). Any attempt to attack France via Belgium, so avoiding the Maginot Line, would be met with the combined might of the French and Belgian armies. However, in 1936 Belgium reverted to a position of strict

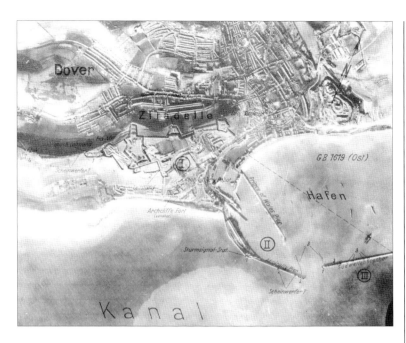

In preparation for operations against Britain the Luftwaffe took a number of aerial photographs of the port of Dover. This one was taken on 20 November 1939. Important features were noted, including the 9.2in. guns of Citadel Battery. By August 1940 the ancient fortifications of the town had been reinforced with AT obstacles, to form an AT barrier that protected the landward approaches. (NJCP)

neutrality and was unwilling to enter into any defensive agreements with France or Britain lest this provoke Germany. Whilst the Dyle Plan (essentially the creation of a defensive line along the River Dyle to counter an expected repeat of the German World War I *Schlieffen* Plan) envisaged a movement into Belgium of a Franco-British force, this could not be undertaken until Belgium 'invited' France and the BEF to move, which would only take place following an invasion. The invitation came at the start of the German attack on Belgium and Holland on 10 May 1940 when the BEF and the French Army moved towards positions on the Dyle Line in Belgium: they did not know that the Wehrmacht would also launch another attack, albeit with some difficulty, further south through the Ardennes to cross the River Meuse at Sedan. Once over the river, the German armoured forces irrupted across northern France: the Allies' lack of both defence in depth and a strategic counter-attack reserve allowed the Germans to cut them in two. If this was not bad enough, trust and co-operation between the French, Belgian and British armies were poor from the outset and grew worse as setback followed setback.

The French High Command suffered from appalling communications facilities: its HQ at Vincennes possessed no wireless centre, telephone landlines were constantly being broken by enemy action, and, perforce, it was largely serviced by motorcycle couriers. Its commander, Gen. Gamelin, was barely on speaking terms with his next in command, Gen. Georges. The BEF, led by Lord Gort VC, was under the command of the French, although Gort had instructions that, in the event of any order gravely affecting the interests of the BEF, he was to refer to British government. He would use this degree of independence when he unilaterally withdrew his forces from Arras in order to block a possible German advance on Dunkirk. This was the one significant counter-attack by the British that resulted in a setback in the Germans' otherwise unhindered move to Abbeville and the coast. Like his French superiors, Gort failed to appreciate the full importance of military intelligence and communications. He split off sections of his command and deprived himself of military intelligence by posting his Director of Military Intelligence, Maj. Gen. Mason-MacFarlane, to lead a field force. The need for military intelligence and effective communications would be a lesson heeded by the military authorities defending Britain in 1940 and 1941 with the establishment of the GHQ Liaison Regiment, also known as 'Phantom'.

On the coast of occupied France, a German soldier armed with an MG34 configured for LAA use looks towards England.

Despite much criticism by the French of Gort's moves after the action at Arras, and general doubts about his abilities, his decisive action enabled the evacuation of almost a quarter of a million exhausted British soldiers together with 100,000 French troops from the beaches of Dunkirk between May 26 and June 4. The operation, codenamed DYNAMO, was directed by Adm. Ramsay from the tunnels beneath Dover Castle. Most of the French troops would eventually be repatriated although a small number would remain and be known as the Fighting Free French under the leadership of Col. Charles de Gaulle. The military disaster had, at least, been mitigated by the evacuation of so many men but the loss of most of the BEF's heavy weaponry, especially tanks and AT guns, made Britain desperately vulnerable. The events of May and June 1940 would mark a low point in Franco-British relations with many mutual recriminations. Now Britain would have to face Germany alone: it would become known as the country's 'finest hour'.

Vigorous fighting between the Germans, French and elements of the BEF to the south of the Somme (the Weygand Line) would continue well into June, the German forces suffering significant losses of men and armour. However, the departure of the main body of the BEF from Dunkirk together with a large section of the northern French Army, signalled a fatal blow to morale. On 14 June Paris fell, and on 22 June 1940 the French Government signed an armistice. Having fought so bravely in World War I to avoid occupation, France would now have to face the humiliation of German control. All of the Atlantic coast and the greater part of France would be occupied by the Germans whilst the south-eastern part would be left under the government of a World War I hero, Marshal Petain, established in the town of Vichy.

Germany's next move was against an isolated part of the British Isles. After an air raid on Jersey on 28 June 1940, which left 34 civilians dead, German forces landed on and occupied the undefended Channel Islands. This would be the only British territory to be occupied by the Germans in World War II, and the experience of the islanders under occupation is now seen as representative of what would have happened to the rest of Britain had it been successfully invaded and occupied too. In addition, the Germans would turn the islands into a fortress. The island of Alderney, for example, would be depopulated and its heavy guns would dominate not only the English Channel but also American supply routes on the Cotentin Peninsula in July 1944. Alderney had the misfortune of containing the only concentration camp on British soil. Lager Sylt, part of a continental complex of camps, held inmates working, like others on the islands, as slave labourers on its defences. The islands were bypassed by the D-Day landings and would stay in German hands until their surrender at the close of the European war in May 1945. By then the German garrison was reduced to virtual starvation whilst the slightly more fortunate islanders were maintained by Red Cross food parcels.

Operation SEALION

The fall of France and the Low Countries and the entry of Italy into the war in the summer of 1940 posed a grave threat to Britain. The BEF's losses in the retreat to Dunkirk (comprising nearly 500 tanks, 40,000 other vehicles, 400 AT guns, and 1,000 heavy guns, together with vast amounts of ammunition and lighter weapons) would take time to replace, and came at a time when they were sorely needed to repulse the expected invader. Now, not only was the German Army massing across the Channel but her bombers could reach all of Britain from French and Norwegian bases. The question the country asked itself was not 'will the Nazis invade?' but '*when* will they invade?'

On 2 July 1940 the Oberkommando der Wehrmacht (OKW) issued an instruction stating that the Führer had ordered preparations to be made for the invasion of Britain. On 12 July Gen. Jodl indicated that the first wave of the assault would consist of seven divisions with AA protection creating a wide-fronted bridgehead between Weymouth and Margate. The Oberkommando der Marine (OKM) was to assemble rapidly the barges and other shipping required to transport the first wave together with their fuel, munitions, weapons and transport. Two further waves were planned with reserves for a fourth wave. Three groups would sail: one from Calais (16th Army), a second from Le Havre (9th Army) and the third (6th Army) from Cherbourg. Accompanying the groups would be Panzer and Gebirgsjäger divisions plus the Waffen-SS Totenkopf Division: the latter had been involved in a number of massacres during the fighting in France. A capacity to transport 400,000 tonnes was required, which would mean 800 vessels with an average capacity of 500 tonnes. In the event, Adm. Raeder had to settle for a multiplicity of smaller craft consisting of tugs, barges, pontoons, fishing and motor boats. On 16 July 1940, over a month after

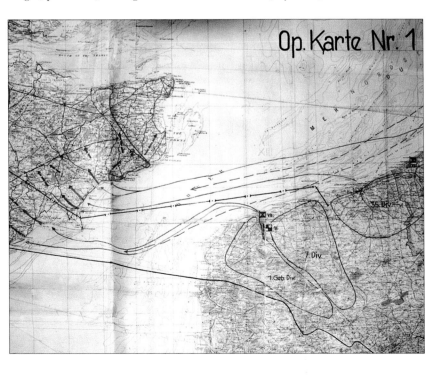

One of several maps prepared by OKW for Operation SEALION showing the shorter landings front of September 1940 between Worthing and Folkestone. Shipping movements are shown from the French and Low Country ports. Note the blue paratrooper symbol to indicate airborne landings around Dover. (Author's photograph, map courtesy of the IWM)

7

the collapse of France, Adolf Hitler issued Directive No. 16 from the Führer HQ, entitled 'On preparations for a landing operation against Britain':

> Since England, in spite of her hopeless military situation, shows no sign of being ready to come to an understanding, I have decided to prepare a landing operation against England and, if necessary, carry it out.
>
> The aim of this operation will be to eliminate the English homeland as a base for the prosecution of the war against Germany and if necessary, to occupy it completely.
>
> I therefore order as follows:
>
> 1. The landing will be in the form of a surprise crossing on a wide front from about Ramsgate to the area west of the Isle of Wight. Units of the airforce will act as artillery and units of the navy as engineers.
>
> The possible advantages of limited operations before the general crossing e.g. the occupation of the Isle of Wight or of the county of Cornwall are to be considered from the point of view of each Branch of the armed forces and the results reported to me. I reserve the decision to myself.
>
> Preparations for the entire operation must be completed by the middle of August.
>
> 2. These preparations must also create such conditions as will make a landing in England possible. Viz:
>
> (a) The English Air Force must be so reduced morally and physically that it is unable to deliver any significant attack against the German crossing.
>
> (b) Mine-free channels must be cleared.
>
> (c) The Straits of Dover must be closely sealed off with minefields on both flanks: also the western entrance to the channel approximately on a line Alderney-Portland.
>
> (d) Strong forces of coastal artillery must command and protect the forward coastal area.
>
> (e) It is desirable that the English Navy be tied down shortly before the crossing, both in the North Sea and in the Mediterranean (by the Italians). For this purpose we must attempt even now to damage English home-based naval forces by air and torpedo attack as far as possible … The attack will bear the cover name 'SEALION'.

At the time of the Directive it can be seen that Hitler was still thinking in very general terms. For example, there is no reference to the number of divisions to be employed. The reference to carrying out the invasion 'if necessary' suggests that he hoped that a diplomatic solution might still be possible, or that Britain might be starved into surrender by an aggressive U-boat and bombing campaign. However, the 66-year-old Winston Churchill, who had succeeded Neville Chamberlain as Prime Minister on 10 May 1940, also taking on the mantle of Minister of Defence, was not a man likely to come to terms with Hitler.

Along the French coast Wehrmacht troops practised the use of assault boats and Gebirgsjäger scaled the chalk cliffs similar to those of the Kent and Sussex coast. In Dutch harbours 2,000 hastily converted barges and coupled pontoons, plus 500 other craft, were brought together to carry the men, tanks and artillery of the invasion force. In addition, as William the Conqueror had found out almost 900 years previously, provision had to be made for the many horses on which the Wehrmacht still relied for moving much of its artillery and supplies. To support the weight of the guns and tanks, concrete was pumped into the bottoms of the barge hulls and sections of the bows were cut away and given ramps and opening doors. To propel the motorless pontoons and slow-moving canal and river barges, aircraft engines were added above their sterns using conversion kits, whilst others were given additional marine engines coupled to complicated drive systems. There were drawbacks though: these vessels could not manoeuvre easily if attacked, and being slow-moving and shallow-draft vessels they could only operate when the Channel was calm and likely to remain so for a period of time (something the British anticipated by devising a range of code words to reflect the different levels of invasion alert). Heavy-calibre railway guns were moved up to the Pas de Calais to target the English beaches with long-range fire and to close the Straits of Dover to British shipping. German fighter and bomber aircraft moved onto captured French airfields along the Channel coast to menace shipping and attempt to wrest control of the skies from the RAF in preparation for invasion.

The task of conducting the invasion fell to Generaloberst Walther von Brauchitsch, whilst the task of co-ordinating the technical aspects of Operation SEALION was given to Gen.

German sailors practice disembarking from a converted barge: the bows have been removed, a false floor fitted and stakes are being positioned to secure the ramp. In the foreground Heer officers confer. (IWM HU 2790)

Georg-Hans Reinhardt. Amongst the interesting and experimental weapons developed for the planned invasion was the UW-Wagen (Unterwasser–Wagen), also known as the U-Panzer: to create this variant, PzKpfw III and IV tanks were modified by adding floating exhaust and air intake tubes and sealing all apertures. The U-Panzer would be launched several hundred metres offshore to travel along the seabed at a depth of up to 15m and then emerge on the opposing beach. Whilst never used operationally for SEALION, the Tauchpanzer III, as it also became known, was used in Operation BARBAROSSA (the invasion of the USSR) when on 22 June 1941 a number of these special tanks successfully crossed the River Bug at Patulin.

As time passed, it became clear that there were differences of opinion within the German high command. The Kriegsmarine favoured a narrower front because it was easier to protect the vulnerable vessels when they were hedged in between the minefields and the groups of U-boats seeking to protect them from the Royal Navy. The Wehrmacht, on the other hand, preferred a broader front stretching from Margate in Kent to Weymouth in Dorset. A compromise was reached between the commands and at the beginning of September the developed plan was to attack on a narrower front from Worthing in Sussex to Folkestone in Kent. The slow-moving armada would sail from ports between Rotterdam and Le Havre and proceed across the Channel in four lines, the pontoons and barges taking up to 15 hours to cross even in calm conditions. Accompanying the troops of the 16th and 9th armies would be three paratrooper regiments – two to drop in the Brighton area, and one to land behind Dover – with the mission to capture and hold inland targets. Maps, based on the British Ordnance Survey, were printed to show the invasion points and breakout routes from the coasts of Sussex and Kent. However, this was predicated by the absolute need to destroy the RAF so that the Luftwaffe would have aerial superiority over the Channel and the beaches.

To enable the invaders to understand the intricacies of British society, SS-Brigadefuhrer Walter Schellenberg of the Nazi Sicherheitsdienst (SD) was instructed in the summer of 1940 to prepare a briefing document that would become infamous, the *Informationsheft GrossBritannien*. In addition to its practical and informative side, the document had a darker side: a list of those that the Gestapo wished to detain and 'deal with' as undesirables. In addition to prominent Jews, the common target of Nazi hatred, the list also included those likely to influence or lead any form of resistance to the occupation.

Developing the defences 1940–41

New forms of warfare

At the beginning of 1940 the British Commander-in-Chief Home Forces was Gen. Kirke. The defence of the country was his responsibility and his first step was to safeguard the major ports from possible capture prior to an invasion. An interim defence plan was prepared as early as February 1940 for the protection of the important port and garrison of Dover in Kent, which also faced the shortest crossing point of the Channel. The defenders were ordered to prepare for a possible attack by way of major landings of enemy troops from the sea, by sabotage parties intent on disrupting the defences, or by attack from airborne forces landing behind the port.

The German campaigns in Norway, the Low Countries and France in the spring and summer of 1940 demonstrated that the enemy's new form of warfare, known as Blitzkrieg, would require new forms of defensive preparation. The simple measures envisaged by Kirke would need drastic revision. Novel, flexible and daring tactics had been used, and Britain would have to take steps to counter them. Some of the innovative assault methods are listed below:

(1) seeking out weak spots in defences by the use of fast, motorised reconnaissance parties and light reconnaissance aircraft;
(2) effective co-operation between tanks and infantry, and the encouragement of a flexible command structure;
(3) tactical co-operation between the Luftwaffe and Wehrmacht, especially using the Junkers Ju 87 Stuka, to eliminate strong points, command centres, armour and troop concentrations;
(4) the deliberate bombing of civilian centres in order to block allied movements and to terrorise the civilian population who would, in fleeing, further obstruct troop movement along main roads;
(5) using aircraft to psychologically destabilise the enemy by delivering troops *behind* their lines (by parachute, glider, seaplane, or by landing Junkers Ju 52/3m transport aircraft on roads and even airfields). Small parties of troops for special missions had also been implanted behind the lines by the use of Fieseler Fi 156 Storch short take-off aircraft.

The attack on Rotterdam in May 1940 provides examples of the above in action. Paratroops were dropped inside the city's football stadium: they then coolly commandeered tramcars to take them into the centre of the city. Twelve Heinkel He 59 seaplanes of Staffel Schwilben landed on the River Maas to deposit 120 troops, who then seized the river bridges. An equally bold attempt to capture the Dutch Royal Family and the Government using Fallschirmäger only failed because the Dutch had previously captured the plans of the operation.

The Home Guard is formed

To deal with the problem of airborne German troops, to expand available manpower and to give time for the Regular Army to retrain and re-equip, on 14 May 1940, the same day that Sedan fell, a quarter of a million men answered the Secretary of State for War's call to join the newly created Local Defence Volunteers. This was soon to be renamed, on Churchill's insistence, the Home Guard. The legality of this citizen's army was established by the passing of the 'Defence (Local Defence Volunteers) Regulations 1940' on 17 May 1940 under the terms of the Emergency Powers (Defence) Act, 1939. The volunteers

---

The government in exile

The likelihood of invasion and the parlous position of the country's defences led in 1940 to the consideration of how the war might be carried on if London fell. Elements of the Admiralty and the Air Ministry, together with essential institutions such as the BBC and the Bank of England, were moved out of London and into the Midlands in 1940. Many large country houses and private schools were requisitioned for this purpose as well as a number of new office complexes. In addition to being King of England, George VI was also Emperor of India and head of the Empire and Commonwealth. It was thus planned that the Royal Family and presumably much of the Cabinet and heads of the armed forces would withdraw northwards if London and the south of England fell. Large houses such as Madresfield Court in Worcestershire and Pitchford Hall in Shropshire were earmarked and provisioned as residences for the monarchy and their retinue as they made their way towards a west coast port for departure to Canada. They would have travelled in Humber 'Ironside' armoured cars, escorted by Coldstream Guards of the 'Coats Mission', named after the officer commanding the column. After the fall of Britain, the Commonwealth and Empire would have carried on the war from Canada.

initially lacked any vestige of weaponry or uniform, apart from privately owned shotguns, but their perceived primary role was to observe and report sightings of paratroopers. To further conduct the hunt for this illusory foe, horse-mounted patrols were established in the remoter parts of the UK, for example along the Welsh border, on Dartmoor and on Exmoor. At this stage of the war newspapers would also refer to them as 'Parashots'. By the late-summer of 1940 the number of men who had joined the Home Guard had reached almost one million.

The birth of the stop-lines

On 27 May 1940 Gen. Kirke was replaced by Gen. 'Tiny' Ironside. By this stage, the fearful effects of Blitzkrieg had been witnessed and analysed. For the defence of over 400 miles of coastline suitable for landing troops and tanks, Ironside possessed only one weak and one incompletely equipped armoured division plus 15 inexperienced infantry divisions with half of their manpower, and possessing only one-sixth of their allotted field guns. The potential front line was also twice as long as the one in France where Germany had faced 80 French and British divisions, aided by the shield of the Maginot Line. To illustrate the paucity of arms, the First London Division, protecting a vital stretch of 70 miles of coastline in Kent, had only 23 field guns, no AT guns and no medium machine guns and a fraction of their allotted AT rifles.

Gen. 'Tiny' Ironside reported his intentions for the defence of the country to the War Cabinet in June and so began the largest scheme of defences the country had ever seen. Because his reserves were so inadequate following the loss of tanks and guns at Dunkirk, his plan was that the enemy would be delayed by beach defences and then 'corralled' by a series of inland AT stop-lines. Once the enemy was delayed within this system, and the direction of attack had been established, reserves would rush forward to counter-attack. To further inhibit the enemy's room for manoeuvre, important communication centres (known as nodal points) would be turned into AT islands. It had been noted that in the fighting for Warsaw the Germans had lost many tanks. The Panzers would not be able to roam at will and create the sense of panic that had previously gripped most of Western Europe. Ironside's system of defence involved the digging of miles of AT ditches in those areas where existing features such as rivers or canals could not provide a barrier, together with the erection of thousands of pillboxes by the Army or by civilian contractors. The creation of AT obstacles, beach defences and obstructions, the laying of thousands of mines and the erection of barbed-wire entanglements proceeded apace.

In addition, all possible aircraft landing sites were obstructed and the airfields had their defences improved. Where would the enemy land? The southern and eastern shores of England seemed most likely and it was in these areas that the heaviest defences were sited. The GHQ stop-line, designed to hold up any German advance on London or the Midlands from the south and east, received the greatest concentration of defences. Other major stop-lines such as the Taunton stop-line protected key cities, in this case the approaches to Bristol from the west. Liverpool and London, together with other major cities, received their own inner and outer stop-lines.

These wartime German postage stamps illustrate elements of Blitzkrieg warfare. The 5 pfennig stamp illustrates a motorcycle reconnaissance unit; the 8 pfennig shows engineers building a bridge across a watercourse. The 20 pfennig features the 2cm Flak, protecting ground forces. The 25 pfennig has a Junkers Ju 87 Stuka carrying out a pinpoint attack, while the 30 pfennig shows Fallschirmjäger troops being dropped from a Junkers Ju 52/3m. The 40 pfennig stamp features an assault by Panzer forces.

Men of the Gloucestershire Regiment parade in front of the Norman castle at Ludlow, Shropshire, September 1940. They are resting and retraining in anticipation of invasion following the evacuation from Dunkirk. In the foreground are two 'knife-rest' roadblocks and in the background the regimental band is playing. (IWM H 3779)

A freshly constructed section of AT ditch, part of the GHQ Line, in the Farnham (Surrey) district, July 1940. Wooden stakes have been driven into the scarped side to prevent soil slippage. Behind the two soldiers various materials are visible, including bundles of stakes. To the left of them is a large concrete AT block. (IWM H 2473)

Ironside's reliance on a series of linear stop-lines might be seen to reflect his experience of war on the Western Front in World War I where such linear trench systems lines had held back the Germans. Now they would have to bar the way of enemy tanks and attempt to box them in to prevent the free movement of German armour and troops witnessed in France 1940.

As a further defensive measure, refugees would be kept off strategic routes required for the rapid movement of home forces and reserves, if necessary by draconian means. The likelihood of diversionary raids in other areas could not be discounted and as long as Eire remained neutral, there remained the possibility of a German invasion there as a precursor to an invasion of Wales. To confuse the enemy all signposts and railway station signs were removed, a situation that continued to make life difficult for UK travellers until later in the war. Petrol stocks would be destroyed and civilian vehicles immobilised to prevent them falling into enemy hands as had happened in France.

Alan Brooke takes over, July 1940

Churchill ordered the retirement of Ironside on 19 July 1940, and Gen. Sir Alan Brooke was given command of Home Forces the following day. Churchill had been unhappy with the performance of his generals, whom he considered to be far less effective than and lacking the imagination of their German counterparts. A policy of bringing in new men who had had first-hand experience of modern warfare in France came to the fore.

The principal architects of the defence of Britain: Winston Churchill and, directly behind him, Gen. Alan Brooke C-in-C Home Forces, photographed in September 1940. On the far right is Gen. Sir John Dill, Chief of the Imperial General Staff. (IWM H 4111).

Like his contemporary Montgomery, Brooke was a believer in a more fluid defence policy, and this led to a change in defensive thinking. Brooke favoured a less static approach with more emphasis on offensive action. In addition, defence in depth would be achieved by the rapid development of an intricate, countrywide system of AT islands and defended localities. Churchill had seen the need to hold the coast, and initially favoured a strong central reserve, believing that the Germans would attack on a wide front. Alan Brooke persuaded him that effort must be put not only into holding the beaches but also into providing an effective reserve close to the coasts. This was all very well, but the country at that time had an inadequate supply of trained and effective troops. On 9 July 1940 Churchill was told by his Chief of Staff, Gen. Ismay, that the country was so short of troops that large areas of the coast together with inland areas had no garrisons. He was in desperate need for a further six divisions for his reserve. It is hardly surprising that at the same time Ismay chided Churchill for the plan to move trained troops to defend India: fortunately Churchill saw the logic of the argument and stayed his hand. Most commands had only one infantry division in reserve and the GHQ Reserve contained only the 2nd Armoured Division plus a small number of miscellaneous divisions and groups undergoing training. The Army had lost much of its motorised transport and as a means of moving the reserve, local bus and coach firms were retained and their vehicles pressed into use as personnel carriers for the mobile counter-attack columns.

The construction of pillboxes slowed as as result of this tactical change of direction: there was also now the problem of conflicting demands for and shortages in building materials. Whilst work on stop-lines and pillboxes would continue into 1941 and beyond, with more equipment and trained troops becoming available, Brooke focused now on developing and increasing his mobile reserve. It was also realised that the tying up of troops along stop-lines or in isolated, vulnerable and inadequately armed pillboxes was a dangerous policy and also a waste of scarce resources: there was also the fundamental problem that there were just not enough troops to adequately man all of the countrywide defences. Taking home defence troops off the building of defences gave them more time for vital training. Eventually, however, the Home Guard would take over the defence of their own localities, freeing much of the Army from these anti-invasion duties.

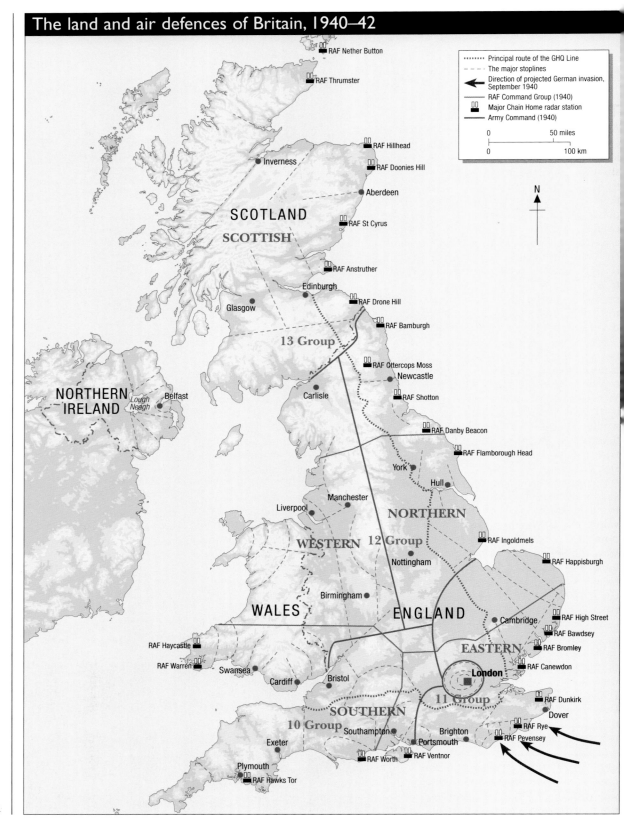

The land and air defences of Britain, 1940–42

Legend:
- •••••• Principal route of the GHQ Line
- – – – The major stoplines
- ← Direction of projected German invasion, September 1940
- —— RAF Command Group (1940)
- ■ Major Chain Home radar station
- —— Army Command (1940)

0 ——— 50 miles
0 ——— 100 km

N

RAF Nether Button

RAF Thrumster

RAF Hillhead

RAF Doonies Hill

Inverness

Aberdeen

SCOTLAND
SCOTTISH

RAF St Cyrus

RAF Anstruther

Edinburgh

Glasgow

RAF Drone Hill

RAF Bamburgh

13 Group

RAF Ottercops Moss

Newcastle

NORTHERN
IRELAND

Lough Neagh

Belfast

Carlisle

RAF Shotton

RAF Danby Beacon

RAF Flamborough Head

York

Hull

Liverpool

Manchester

NORTHERN

12 Group

RAF Ingoldmels

Nottingham

RAF Happisburgh

Birmingham

WESTERN

WALES

ENGLAND

Cambridge

RAF High Street

RAF Bawdsey

EASTERN

RAF Bromley

RAF Haycastle

RAF Warren

Swansea

Cardiff

Bristol

RAF Canewdon

London

11 Group

RAF Dunkirk

Dover

SOUTHERN

10 Group

Southampton

Brighton

RAF Rye

RAF Pevensey

Portsmouth

Exeter

RAF Worth

RAF Ventnor

Plymouth

RAF Hawks Tor

Britain's land defences

The Home Guard

After much initial confusion, the Home Guard's primary role would eventually evolve as observation, reporting and the defence of their towns, villages and localities. They knew these areas intimately and it was only natural that they should defend them. In addition to this primary role they would also form reconnaissance patrols and fighting patrols to destroy small enemy parties in their vicinity as long as this did not clash with their primary role. The need to prevent the passage of enemy reconnaissance parties, or the mythical fifth columnists, led to the construction by the Home Guard of many roadblocks around the country. Manned by the civilian police when routine identity checking was carried out and protected by the Home Guard, these checks were resented by civilians and members of the armed forces alike and a number of fatalities occurred when the Home Guard became over-zealous. Often badly sited and as much of an obstruction to the Army as to the Germans, their numbers would eventually be reduced substantially: many badly sited defence positions from the same 1940 period would also be removed.

The first Home Guard 'uniform' consisted of crudely made LDV armbands, but soon stocks of redundant Army denim overall battledress blouses and trousers became available. It was impossible, however, for the volunteers, many of whom had served in Kitchener's army in World War I, or even in the Boer War, to look smart in this baggy apparel. It was quite quickly replaced by battledress of khaki serge so that the appearance of the Home Guardsman would be similar to his Regular Army counterpart. The responsibility for 'kitting-out' rested with the officials of the Territorial Army Association. They were much criticised and those members of the Home Guard of non-average shape often had a long wait for items such as greatcoats.

In terms of the weaponry that the Home Guard possessed, the shotgun, with solid shot and a lethal range of 50 yards, would remain in Home Guard use up to stand-down in the winter of 1944. Once America realised that the country would put up a fight against Hitler, she was agreeable to selling substantial numbers of weapons to Britain from August 1940. Other weapons, such as the Ross rifle, would come from Canada.

By the late-summer of 1940 only half of the million-strong Home Guard possessed rifles, and those that did had little ammunition (usually only five rounds). The standard rifle was the US-made .30in. M1917 (Enfield), known to the Home Guard as the P17. Most of the rifle ammunition used by the Home Guard was US .30in. calibre. Using the British .303in. round led to the American rifles jamming: a red band was therefore painted around the rifles as a reminder to use the correct ammunition. A large number of US .45in. Thompson submachine guns was also received, to be exchanged in 1942 for the

BELOW Men of the No.4 Warwickshire Local Defence Volunteers pose proudly by their armoured car in 1940 – a civilian car or van chassis covered in steel plate for protection. No uniforms have yet been issued, just LDV armbands, and they appear to be armed with the Lee-Enfield Mk III rifle. Note that the local vicar is part of the platoon. (CET)

The Home Guard practice with the Northover Projector in September 1941: note the 'HG' tab on the epaulette of the figure in the foreground. The seated figure operates the trigger whilst the crouching figure holds a No. 36 M grenade. This appears to have a gas seal around its base and is ready for loading into the breech of the Projector. (IWM H 11843)

crude 9mm Sten submachine gun. The eventual availability of Lewis machine guns, together with US Browning automatic rifles and medium machine guns, gave them more firepower.

By the middle of the war the Home Guard had received from the Army the obsolete 2pdr AT gun together with sub-artillery such as the Smith Gun. These would have been effective against soft-skinned and lightly armoured vehicles but less so against the up-armoured PzKpfw IV tank. The heavier German tanks, such as the Panther, would have to be tackled by the larger AT mines or the Army's 6pdr or 17pdr AT guns. The Home Guard was also issued with a small AT mine, the No. 75 grenade (also known as the Hawkins grenade), which, when used in clusters, was quite capable of disabling a medium tank. Among the other weapons in its arsenal was the Flame Fougasse: this comprised a barrel of inflammable liquid that was ignited by a SIP grenade. It was positioned by road blocks, situated in defiles, ready to project a sheet of flame upon anyone or anything on the other side of the obstruction.

Adequately arming the Home Guard was a slow process. In the summer of 1941 the notorious Home Guard pike was issued. By this time the volunteers were becoming fully armed and the circumstances surrounding the issue of this medieval-like weapon are obscure. It consisted of an obsolete sword-type rifle bayonet rammed into a length of steel tubing. Most quartermasters wisely decided to leave this weapon on their shelves.

The development of defensive doctrine

Maj. Tom Wintringham, through polemical articles in the influential *Picture Post* magazine, campaigned for the better training of the relatively new Home Guard. He had served in the British Army in World War I, edited the Communist *Daily Worker* between the world wars, and had served in a senior position in the International Brigade in the Spanish Civil War, becoming commander of the British Battalion and later an instructor in the Officers' School. Wintringham felt that it was his duty, in the fight against fascism, to put his experiences in the recent Spanish war at the disposal of the Home

A 29mm Spigot Mortar on a mobile mounting: a practice bomb is being loaded into the mortar (right). The photograph was taken at the No. 3 Home Guard Training School at Stokesay Court in Shropshire in 1943. The men on the left wear extemporised camouflage. It is possible that the officer second from the right is Maj. Tom Wintringham. (IWM H 30180)

Guard. Together with other Spanish Civil War veterans, he founded a training school at Osterley Park near London. Distrusted by Churchill, who was vehemently anti-Communist, the school was soon taken over by the War Office, but Wintringham and the others were not re-employed. The institution of Osterley Park would lead to the establishment of three GHQ Home Guard training schools, together with large numbers of specialised training schools, including street-fighting schools.

Much of what Wintringham taught and wrote about in his books *New Ways of War* and *Peoples' War* (published between 1940 and 1942) was absorbed by the War Office. Wintringham, it seems, received little acknowledgement because of his political leanings, although he and other Osterley Park instructors would, eventually, return to play a role in passing on their skills to the new Home Guard schools. He was critical of anachronistic practices such as bayonet drill, 'spit and polish' and what he saw as the amateurish aspects of Home Guard battle instruction. The more unusual aspects of his influence can be seen in the War Office's recommendation of the use of cloth screens to be stretched across village or town streets, and the use of upturned soup plates, pretending to be AT mines. It was optimistically hoped that upon encountering these devices German tanks would slow or halt and thus be easier for Home Guard tank-hunting teams to attack.

Tom Wintringham's *New Ways of War*, published in 1940, advocated the concept of 'a people's war'. His books and writings in the periodical *Picture Post* were influential in drawing attention to the need for innovative tactics when tackling new forms of warfare. (PB)

Daily life in the Home Guard

Life for the average Home Guardsman, as it was for those men and women in Civil Defence, was hard. In addition to carrying out his full time work he was expected to turn out for parades, field exercises, instruction and weapon training in his spare time. The Home Guard used a range of weapons, all of which required instruction, and marksmanship training was vital too. For the officers there was a mass of paperwork flowing from Zone HQs down to the battalions and platoons and back again. Training had to be organised and supervised. Whilst one Shropshire platoon, for example, on formation in May 1940 consisted of 'old soldiers, sailors, cripples, youngsters and the local parson', by 1942 the organisation was becoming more effective and at the time of the D-Day landings the Home Guard could be entrusted with the defence of the kingdom. Maurice Winnell of Macclesfield in Cheshire, a young and fit man who would go to war with the Royal Artillery in 1942, remembers the keenness of his colleagues in his local battalion who, he was sure, would have given

the Germans a hard time. Many of the Home Guard had seen action in World War I, were still fit and had had more weapon and combat experience than many Regular Army men. Other members included young men waiting to go into the forces. Whilst the Home Guard never engaged the enemy (apart from on their AA duties), almost 2,500 members died from a variety of causes during service. This remarkable citizen's army was stood down on 3 December 1944. It would be revived briefly a few years later at the time of the Korean War.

TOP One of the pillboxes built by the BEF in 1939–40 at Cysoing in their sector of northern France. This particular design was grouped in fours to cover a French AT ditch. (MO)

BOTTOM The interior of a pillbox at Friston in Suffolk, one of four guarding an important road junction. It was built by the Royal Engineers in August 1940 (note the date over the doorway) using concrete block forms. The very simple and hasty nature of such 1940 defences is exemplified by this work, which lacks any form of internal anti-ricochet wall.

Pillboxes, fortified positions and weaponry

In the summer of 1940, the country's defence rested on holding the beaches for as long as possible and delaying the enemy and his tanks by stop-lines and carefully sited pillboxes. The pillboxes, often ingeniously camouflaged by the efforts of artists and stage designers such as Oliver Messel, provided a protected strongpoint of concrete or brick-faced concrete for a squad of men armed with the .303in. Bren light machine gun, the Boys .55in. AT rifle and .303in. Lee-Enfield rifles.

The British defensive commanders put much faith in the pillbox: its principal drawback was that its high and angular silhouette was easily spotted. In addition, most were unable to resist high-explosive projectiles and the provision of openings on all sides made them vulnerable to accurate fire. It is also likely that the forward Wehrmacht elements would have riddled any building or defensive feature with machine-gun, 2cm light Flak, 3.7cm AT and 7.5cm infantry howitzer fire. The Germans had dealt with the immeasurably

Anti-invasion defences were not just built in the countryside. Here a cleverly camouflaged pillbox (by the side of the tall man) has been built to cover Westminster Bridge and Victoria Embankment, London. The Houses of Parliament are to the left whilst Westminster Abbey is in the background. The photograph was taken in September 1940. (IWM H 3476)

Another ingeniously camouflaged pillbox: it is a pity that the large concrete block, restricting the road width, gives the game away! To its right, sockets for steel AT rails have been fitted. This photograph was taken in October 1940. (IWM H 4774)

stronger Maginot Line fortifications by using the tactic of destroying the 'eyes' of the forts (the armoured steel observation cupolas) using the deadly 88mm dual-purpose gun. It follows that they would have had little difficulty in taking out the British pillbox, although it is interesting to note that in April 1941 GHQ Home Forces considered a design for a pillbox proof against the 88mm gun. This monster would have had walls up to six-feet-thick and would have been difficult if not impossible to conceal. The external walls of most pillboxes, featuring between one- and two-feet-thick concrete, were only proof against rifle calibre ammunition: in March 1940 Alan Brooke noted that the small French Hotchkiss 25mm AT gun used in limited numbers by the BEF could penetrate two feet of reinforced concrete. Some reinforced pillboxes, featuring concrete walls three and a half feet thick, were deemed 'shell-proof' by the War Office.

The Army was also conscious of the risk from flame-throwers and other weapons of the German assault engineers, so barbed-wire entanglements were placed around pillboxes to keep assault weapons out of range: nearby weapon pits would also provide further protection for the position. Where only enemy infantry was involved, pillboxes armed with rifles and Bren light-machine guns would put up a spirited defence and delay the movement of infantry significantly as they attempted to cross stop-lines and other defended areas.

In addition to defending the stop-lines, pillboxes were also built to form part of the ground defences of airfields as well as radar, AA, coast artillery or searchlight sites and would be manned by the troops from the sites. In June 1940 a range of designs for the pillboxes was prepared by the War Office's Directorate of Fortifications and Works to provide for a variety of tactical situations. There ensued a myriad of local variations designed by Royal Engineer companies and RAF Works departments and made from a variety of materials. As wooden shuttering became scarcer, brick shuttering was used instead. Others had pre-formed concrete sides, their interiors filled with weak concrete. Other designs, such as the steel Allan Williams Turret, had a brief life, as steel became scarce. Many different designs appeared for use on airfields, perhaps the most ingenious being the Pickett-Hamilton Fort, a retractable pillbox, elevated by hydraulic or manual means. It was found to be unreliable and too lightly armed, and the design was therefore not popular with the RAF.

Larger structures were designed to hold the Vickers machine gun or the 2pdr AT gun (the latter in very short supply after Dunkirk; Ironside had only 170 at his disposal), or the 6pdr Hotchkiss QF (quick firing) Mk II improvised AT gun. It is believed that more positions were built than there were guns available: on alert the guns would have been rushed from a central depot to wherever they were needed. Some 6pdr positions consisted merely of a concrete base together with the bolts onto which the gun would have been secured. Possibly a protection of sandbags was intended for these exposed guns. Other weapons used briefly in the AT role, but probably not provided with concrete positions, were the 4in. gun and the famous French 75mm gun, the latter from US stocks.

The most acute problem in 1940 was the chronic lack of 2pdr AT guns, a weapon that was, in any event, becoming obsolete. The improvised Hotchkiss 6pdr QF Mk II gun, firing solid shot, was rushed into service and remained so until early 1941 when it was passed to the Home Guard. They fitted the gun onto a small two-wheeled carriage to serve as a mobile AT gun. This shortage of guns led to the desperate expedient of ordering the Regular Army, and also the Home Guard, to make their own AT weapons. 'Molotov Cocktails', made from beer or whisky bottles filled with locally obtained tar, petrol and paraffin, were produced in large numbers: these weapons had been used in Spain and Finland. When the bottles broke (hopefully against an enemy tank) the mixture would be ignited by two special matches attached to the bottle and lit before the bottle was thrown. If thrown in sufficient numbers it was hoped that they would disable the tank's engine or kill or injure the crew. The problem was that a soldier had to get very close to the tank and risked being killed by supporting infantry fire or the tank's own guns.

A slightly more sophisticated form of Molotov was the No.76 Grenade, also known as the SIP (self-igniting phosphorous) or AW Bomb (Albright and Wilson were the manufacturers). This, too, consisted of a glass bottle filled with an inflammable mixture, with the addition of a strip of latex to give adhesion on the surface of the tank. Ignition was by means of a small quantity of phosphorous separated from the other ingredients by a layer of water. The breaking of the bottle caused the phosphorous to ignite on contact with the air, igniting in turn the inflammable mixture. Another AT weapon was the No.74 Grenade, known as the Sticky Bomb. This consisted of a flask of

An obviously posed photograph of a Home Guard exercise. The men are armed with US .30 M1917 (Enfield) rifles and crouch behind AT 'hairpin' obstacles. These have been given blackout markings (the white stripes), as it is likely they would have been stacked at the roadside or on the pavement. Of interest is the cloth screen, designed to confuse and confound enemy armour as to what lay beyond. The photograph was taken in September 1942. (IWM H 24019)

nitro-glycerine attached to a handle. Surrounding the flask was an adhesive substance, which served to attach the bomb to the tank before detonation. There were various obvious weaknesses in its design, such as an alarming tendency for the explosive to leak out of the flask, and it was eventually withdrawn.

The lack of AT artillery in 1940 also led to the invention of a number of ingenious pieces of sub-artillery, all of which bore the name of the inventor. Although the intention of the inventors was that these might equip the Army and RAF ground units, in the event the Home Guard was the major and grateful recipient. These weapons, in addition to the 2pdr AT gun eventually relinquished by the Army, would form the Home Guard's principal AT capability. Perhaps the most basic weapon was the Northover Projector, known to the War Office as the Projector, 2.5in., which consisted of a smoothbore barrel together with a hinged breech, and standing on a four-legged base. This short-range weapon fired either the No. 76 Grenade (SIP) for AT use or the No.36M Grenade for anti-personnel (AP) work. The weapon could also fire the rare No.68 Grenade, which used the hollow-charge principle for AT work. Propulsion of the grenades was by means of a wallet of black powder ignited by a percussion cap inserted in the breech block.

Rather better made, but more expensive to produce, was the Smith Gun, also known as the 3in. OSB (Ordnance Smooth Bore). The barrel was placed between two large solid wheels and was provided with a shield. When upturned the gun rested on the concave wheel with the convex wheel providing a degree of overhead cover. This compact arrangement hindered mobility over rough ground, however, and in urban fighting it was recommended that toggle ropes, supplied to the Home Guard, should be used to manhandle the weapon into position. This was a weapon for the younger and fitter members of the Home Guard: being rather large, it was also a difficult weapon to conceal. Firing either a 6lb hollow-charge AT bomb or an 8lb AP bomb, the Smith Gun was seen to be less effective than the Northover Projector or the 29mm Spigot Mortar.

The Spigot Mortar, also known as the Blacker Bombard, is perhaps the best known weapon in this category. Although designed with mobility in mind, the weapon was heavy, the mortar alone weighing 112lb. It could be positioned on a large cruciform base, or fired from a static concrete pedestal on which sat a stainless steel pivot. As the pivot was considered to be part of the gun, surviving

A pillbox under construction in September 1940, contained within a damaged building for camouflage. Covers have been fitted over the loopholes and over one of these a false window has been fitted. To the right, road sockets are being constructed and on either side of these metal obstacles have been positioned. The iron rails that would have been fitted into the sockets to form an AT barrier are positioned far right. (IWM H 3539)

Defending an AT island

This hypothetical scene shows the principles of how the Home Guard might defend the outer approaches to an AT island. No. 75 (Hawkins) grenades, wired together on a sledge, have been pulled across the road to break the tracks of enemy tanks. Home Guardsmen have occupied a fortified house. Other Guardsmen, from the cover of a wall, throw SIP grenades at the disabled tank, setting the engine on fire. A Spigot Mortar engages the following tank, striking and dislodging the turret mechanism. A Browning Automatic Rifle (BAR) gives protection to the mortar position and engages enemy infantry, as does a Browning medium machine gun concealed behind a loopholed wall. Rifle fire comes from 'mouseholes' in the walls of the fortified house whilst other men are ready with grenades at the wire-meshed upper windows.

A   Triple barbed wire
B   Sledge rope
C   Spigot Mortar pit
D   BAR weapon pit, with sandbag
    protection
E   Browning medium machine gun,
    under camouflage net, with two
    riflemen for support
F   Home Guard with SIP grenades
G   Home Guard sniper in spire

The inset illustration, based on a Home Guard training manual, demonstrates the principles of and positions taken within the fortified house.

i   Bomber
ii   Sniper/observer
iii   Bomber
iv   Riflemen firing from below
      ground level
v   Cellar filled with ammunition
      and supplies
vi   Guttering and drain pipes
      removed from building
vii   Stairs obstructed by
      barbed wired
viii Squad commander's position,
      with view hole

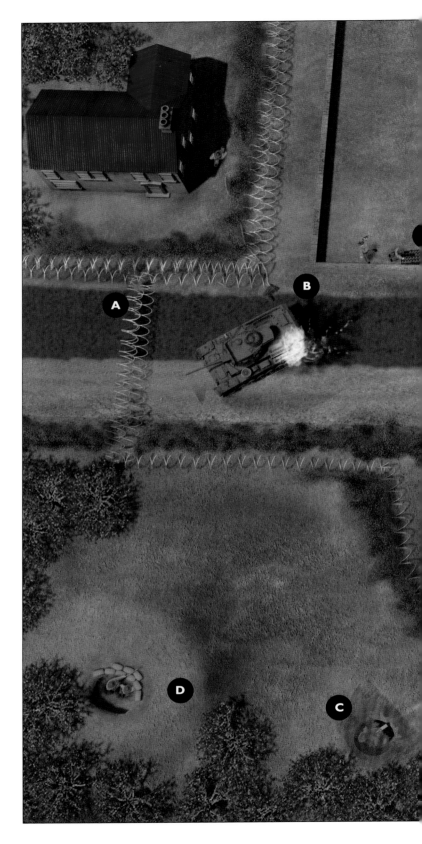

Inside a pillbox emplacement for the Hotchkiss 6pdr Mk II improvised AT gun in October 1940 at Ledsham, Cheshire, forming part of the outer defences of the Birkenhead area. Above the gun is a small range-card with local features marked. The soldiers are from the 98th Field Regiment RA (Surrey) Yeomanry. (IWM H 4533)

examples will be found to have proof markings. The pedestal was usually situated in a weapon pit with lockers for ammunition. In the static role, the mortar would cover a known feature, for example a roadblock on a bridge. As it was muzzle-loaded, its rate of fire was low (about six rounds per minute for the AT round). It was therefore essential that the first shot counted and that the weapon was adequately camouflaged. Again, two types of round were supplied: the 20lb AT bomb and the 14lb AP bomb. The mortar was primarily an AT weapon and the round for this purpose relied entirely on blast to disable a tank. Within the tail of each bomb a cartridge was fitted; when a spring-loaded spigot (which gave the weapon its name) was released this struck and exploded the cartridge forcing the bomb out of the barrel in a shallow arc. The Army's PIAT (Projector, Infantry, Anti-Tank) weapon, also designed by Lt. Col. Blacker, used a similar system but fired a penetrating hollow-charge bomb.

Thousands of Blacker Bombard positions were built around the country, and many still survive. The Blacker Bombard apparently gave a good account of itself in the AP role in the Western Desert, although both usage of and enthusiasm for the weapon were probably curtailed by its weight. Assuming the weapon could make its first shot count, a 20lb bomb landing on the turret roof or engine deck of most German tanks would have proved calamitous. A hit near the turret ring or on a track idler would be sufficient to immobilise the tank and make it the prey of Home Guard tank-hunting parties armed with the SIP grenade.

As Britain gained strength and confidence with the passing of time, the need for costly and elaborate anti-invasion defences was reviewed. By early 1942 the pillbox, such an icon of the dark times of 1940, had had its day and would henceforth be replaced by easily constructed and flexible field works. Pillboxes would only, in future, be incorporated into local defence schemes if they could be completely concealed, were proof against the heaviest enemy tanks and if their loopholes gave complete and all-round fields of fire. There was also the difficulty of communicating with those inside the pillbox when it was under fire. The opinion also became prevalent that keeping men inside such works did not make for aggressive defence. Redundant pillboxes would also be incorporated into defence plans as decoys, whilst others, made of plasterboard, had been erected in 1940 specifically for this purpose.

Anti-tank islands

With the shift in defensive thinking following Alan Brooke's appointment in July 1940, greater emphasis was placed on a system of defence in depth. From early 1941 the stop-lines would only be manned where the Home Guard could provide a garrison; this meant close to villages where roads crossed a stop-line, or at places where static troops could hold the locality. Henceforth there would now be an extensive countrywide network of defended localities, centres of resistance with all-round defences that would be mutually supporting. By the spring of 1941 all work on inland stop-lines had largely ceased. Faced with the crippling losses of war *matériel* after Dunkirk, the cream of the Army defeated and demoralised, the defenders could only play for time and trade space should a landing be made whilst meagre counter-attack forces manoeuvred, reinforcements were being trained and new equipment produced. The defended localities would be known as anti-tank islands. Each anti-tank island would constitute a tank-killing zone, with the Home Guard using the AT weapons at its disposal. In most of these defended areas, a 'keep' or place of last resort would be identified in the centre of the island, which would also serve as the local defence HQ: normally it would be in a substantial building, such as a town hall. The Home Guard, tasked with defending these locations, were ordered to fight to the last man and the last bullet.

Behind this defensive scheme lay the awareness that, whilst infantry and tanks might leave roads and bypass some of the defended localities, heavy artillery and motor transport needed road systems. Blitzkrieg relied on speed of movement: bypassing obstructions meant delay and so the philosophy was geared to the use of unimpeded roads. As long as the Home Guard could control and hold the major road junctions, river crossing points, towns and cities, the enemy would have to undertake time-consuming diversions. It was also believed that built-up areas would favour the defender, tanks being particularly vulnerable to attack from above by defenders occupying the upper floors of buildings. This was illustrated in the fighting for Warsaw in 1939 when one Panzer regiment lost 57 out of a strength of 120 tanks. Enemy bombing or shelling would merely create blocked roads in towns and cities and would improve the opportunities for creating cover. The future battles at Stalingrad and Caen confirmed these premises.

Anti-tank islands decline, 1942–43

By August 1942 the initial anti-invasion activity had declined to such an extent that Lord Dorchester was moved to write to the War Office stating that despite the large expenditure on turning the town of Reading into an anti-tank island, the defences were still not complete. In addition, those that had been completed were in a state of disrepair. He further claimed that the civilian authorities were clamouring for more co-operation with the military authorities, that there had been little dialogue regarding the role of the civilian agencies in the event of an invasion, and that the military commander had clearly too many responsibilities.

A none-too-young group of Home Guardsmen practice erecting an AT barrier during a Northern Command exercise in November 1941. At least one rail has been placed into a socket (note the socket covers) whilst heavy concrete cylinders are being positioned in threes in front of the rail. The cylinders were designed to impede the movement of a tank attempting to smash through the rails. Rubble would have been scattered about to prevent overturned cylinders being used by a tank as rollers. (IWM H 15192)

Coastal defences

ABOVE The construction of Battery Lindemann at Sangatte, near Calais, one of several batteries built to shell England and to deny use of the Channel to British shipping. The three enormous turreted guns were of 40.6cm calibre.

Throughout 1940, aircraft of RAF Coastal Command together with minesweepers and submarines of the Royal Navy patrolled the British coastline and beyond, alert to the threat from the anticipated Axis armada. Suicidal 'Scarecrow' patrols of groups of de Havilland Tiger Moth and Miles trainers armed with light bombs were prepared to attack enemy troops landing on the beaches: they would have suffered appalling losses from the enemy's flak and fighters. Existing and emergency coastal batteries, in protected positions, and equipped with 4in., 6in. and 9.2in. guns, would attempt to prevent any invasion barges or warships not destroyed by the Royal Navy from approaching the British coast. The same heavy weapons would also be turned to bombard adjacent beaches if landings took place. Inland, World War I vintage heavy howitzers, cumbersome to move and slow to fire, were brought out of storage in order to add to the beach barrage. Even weapons considered to be 'inhumane' were considered for the coastal defence role. Churchill was quite prepared to order the bombing or spraying of any German troops landing on Britain's beaches with poison gas, and fearsome flame weapons were installed from Fowey in Cornwall to Dover in Kent to engulf beach exits in flame. Experiments aimed at covering the sea in burning oil were less successful: the system was very much weather-dependent, the oil was difficult to ignite, and it was eventually considered to be a waste of precious fuel resources. The much quoted and sensational report that in 1940 dozens of burnt German bodies were found on British beaches is believed to have no basis in fact.

OPPOSITE **The 15in. No.1 gun 'Jane', Wanstone Battery, Kent**

The 15in. naval gun 'Jane' (A) was one of two huge guns emplaced at Wanstone Farm (near St Margaret's-at-Cliffe, Kent) in spring 1942: the other was No.2 gun 'Clem', set c. 400m away. The combined firepower of these two weapons, together with the other locally-sited guns Winnie and Pooh, contributed to the cross-Channel duel with the German guns on Cap Gris Nez. The inset map (B) shows the ranges and locations of the guns: Clem and Jane could only dominate the Channel (max range 36,900 yds normal charge, 42,000 yds super charge) whereas Winne and Pooh's 14in. guns had a longer reach (47,250 yds). The guns were manned by the Royal Artillery 540th

Coast Regiment. The No.1 (C) and No. 2 (D) ammunition magazines were protected with earthen covers. The gun had a dedicated power plant (E) next to it: the battery command post (not shown) lay further back. The guns were protected by four 3.7in. HAA guns (F): the command post for the HAA guns is at (G). Air raid shelters were also located in this area. Behind Jane's gun house lay an armoured crane, and a locker for live shells was to the left under a camouflage net supported by concrete pillars (H). The gun was fired from a platform on the right hand side of the gun house. A further inset (I) shows Jane in closer view (some of the camouflage has been removed for clarity). The Wanstone battery was eventually dismantled in 1957.

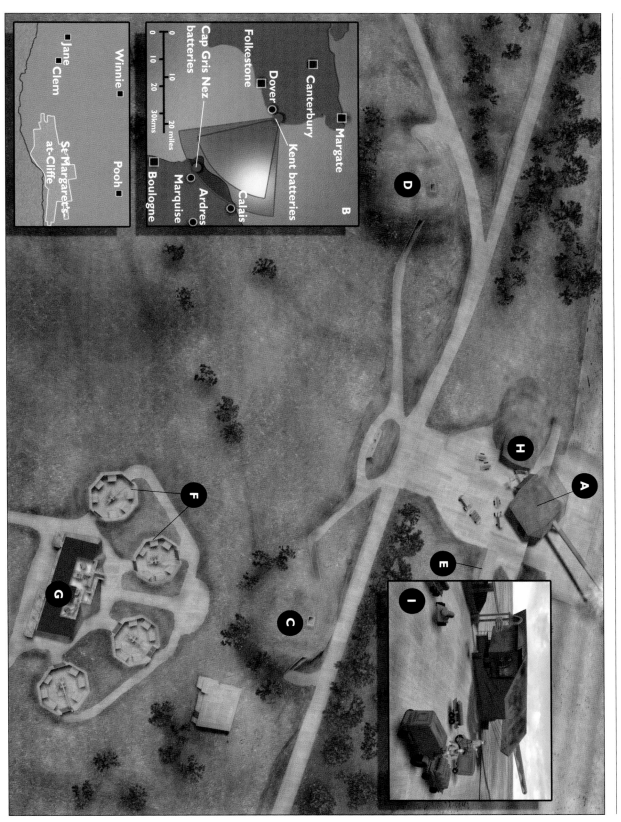

B

Margate

Canterbury

Folkestone

Dover

Cap Gris Nez
batteries

Kent batteries

Ardres

Marquise

Calais

Boulogne

0   10   20   30kms

0   10   20 miles

Winnie

Jane

Clem

St Margaret's-
at-Cliffe

Pooh

Heavy artillery: the coastal big guns

Both the Germans and the British deployed heavy guns that faced each other across the English Channel. The British fielded guns from 9.2in. to the enormous 18in. 'Bochebuster' railway-mounted howitzer of the 11th Super Heavy Battery, Royal Artillery. The super-heavy guns in Kent were installed in response to the German emplacment of heavy guns in the Pas de Calais, which were tasked with denying the Channel to British shipping. The installation of the super-heavy guns was somewhat counter productive, as shots from the Kentish batteries fired at German ships in the Channel provoked the shelling of Dover in response. To a certain extent this warded off further British shelling, although in 1944 the Kent guns would take valedictory revenge by helping the Canadian forces seize the opposing German batteries following the D-Day landings.

Coastal artillery

The need to protect Britain's ports and harbours with artillery stretched back to the days of Henry VIII. The expansion of the British Empire and Navy and the perceived threat from France in the 19th century lead to great advances in artillery, battery and fortress building. In addition, it was possible to close harbour mouths by the use of controlled, sunken minefields, a practice carried into World War II. By 1910, all of Britain's ports had modern coastal artillery batteries emplaced, with Belfast the last to be so provided.

The two principal guns employed in the defences were the 6in. and the 9.2in. guns. The former, in its Mk 7 and Mk 24 models, had ranges of 14,000 and 24,500 yds respectively. The Mk 10 9.2in. gun had a range of 36,700 yards: this gun provided long-range protection for the country's principal naval ports. Coast artillery searchlights (CASL) provided night-time illumination of potential targets.

Fire-control methods in 1940 had changed little since the beginning of the century, relying on optical instruments for range and position finding, and tide tables, with gun fire controlled from a Battery Observation Post (BOP). As the war progressed this situation was revolutionised by the introduction of CA (Coast Artillery) radar: one model was designed for detecting the approach of enemy craft, whilst the other served as a fire-control radar.

The fear of invasion in 1940 led to the building of a large number of Emergency Batteries

The April 1940 invasion of Norway resulted in defensive measures being put in place in the far north of Scotland. These were carried on down the eastern coast of Scotland and into England. This picture shows a camouflaged Hotchkiss 6pdr Mk II improvised AT gun at Druridge Bay on the Northumberland coast, in October 1940. (IWM H 4879)

around the coast armed with any available guns, many ex-naval. The battery emplacements were often crude and exposed to both the elements and enemy fire until such time as hardened gun houses and shelters could be built for the guns, their crews and the ammunition.

The threat from fast German torpedo boats in World War I led to the development of the twin 6pdr coast gun. The mounting appeared before the outbreak of World War II, and it was capable of delivering 120 rounds per minute. Its most famous use in combat was the destruction of an Italian torpedo boat force off Malta in 1941. Although no examples of this equipment remain in Britain, the tall director towers and gun positions remain at sites such as Landguard Battery, Suffolk and Hurst Castle in the Solent.

Area Combined HQ

The move of Western Approaches Command from its potentially vulnerable location in Plymouth to Derby House, Liverpool, was at Churchill's insistence.

Polish troops construct beach defences at Tentsmuir in Fife in November 1940. Some still wear Polish or French Army berets. A long line of AT cubes has been built and behind these is a stake and sandbag AT wall. The pillbox on the right was built to contain a searchlight. Much of this work still survives today. (IWM H 5490)

In his previous capacity as First Sea Lord, he ordered that the specially converted basement of the office building be used as a command HQ. Churchill later admitted that the only thing that frightened him in the war was the U-boat threat. Not only was there to be a naval HQ here but the RAF's Coastal Command, a vital weapon in the Battle of the Atlantic, would be represented too, to form a combined HQ. From the gas and bomb-proof basement over 1,000 personnel, under the overall initial command of Adm. Sir Percy Noble and then most famously Adm. Sir Max Horton, controlled the movement and protection of the convoys carrying vital goods across the Atlantic. At the time of the move to Liverpool in early 1941, Britain was losing more shipping than she could manufacture. The arrival of ship and aircraft mounted radar, improved convoy tactics, long-range aircraft and, finally, the closing of the Atlantic 'gap' following the entry of the US into the war meant that all of the ocean could be effectively protected: the U-boats' 'Happy Times' were over.

One of the few surviving examples of a 6in. coast gun, now emplaced at Newhaven Fort, Sussex. During the war such guns would have received rear, lateral and overhead protection. In the summer of 1940 the only 6in. guns between the ports of Dover and Portsmouth were the four defending the port of Newhaven.

OPPOSITE **Coastal defences at Aldeburgh, Suffolk 1942**
This illustration shows the layout of a typical 'Emergency Battery' position and defended beachhead in 1942. The battery comprises a pair of 6in. coast defence guns (No.1 Gun is at A, and No.2 Gun is at B), which cover the approaches to the beach. Considerable thought was given to the camouflage of coast artillery positions. Often a false roof would be built on top of the gun house and a canvas screen, painted to represent the front of a building, could be drawn across the front and secured with pegs, as shown in the inset image (K). To prevent the gun's shadow giving itself away, it would often be moved to lie parallel with the front of the gun house. The men of the battery were billeted in the hotel next to the No.2 Gun. The guns

formed part of an integrated system of anti-invasion defences. Along the beach and behind the battery and observation post (F), tubular scaffolding has been erected to hinder both landings by boat and troop movements (C). Anti-tank cubes form the next level of protection (D), with concertina barbed wire laid behind them. Naval mines have also been buried in the beach (E). Two coast artillery searchlights illuminate the seaward approaches at night (No.1 is at G, and No.2 is at H). The beach is also protected by a pillbox (I), and also by several Spigot Mortar positions close to the guns. An inset (J) shows the interior of the observation post for the battery, complete with a depression position finder, spotting binoculars and transmitting dial.

Defending Britain's airspace

Throughout the summer and autumn of 1940, observation posts were built and manned from dawn to dusk to watch for paratroop landings, whilst vulnerable points such as telephone exchanges, power stations and radio stations were guarded against seizure or possible acts of sabotage. Broadcast facilities also needed to be heavily guarded to prevent seizure and use by the Germans: in Norway in 1940 the Germans had used them to undermine command and control facilities. False reports of Fallschirmjäger landings were common in the summer months.

RAF airfields and their approaches, which might be used by the enemy, were guarded and protected by ground and AA defences. The airfields were also home to the scarce fighters, bombers and spare parts required for the defence of the country. In the summer of 1940 they were provided with pillboxes arranged around their perimeters. From 1941 onwards, when a more flexible approach to defence was introduced countrywide, major airfields were provided with a reinforced Battle Headquarters tasked with the co-ordination of the defence of the airfield itself and also its approaches. In addition, with the formation of the RAF Regiment in early 1942, the RAF would be able to rely on its own resources and not those of the Army. As the war progressed, there were also changes in airfield design. The pre-war policy of grouping hangars and accommodation on airfields was rejected because it offered too convenient a target to the Luftwaffe and so the camps for the hundreds of RAF and WAAF air and ground crews were dispersed over the surrounding countryside. Hangars, too, were spaced about the grassed or concrete runwayed airfields.

The risk of enemy air landings in other potential locations was also considered a grave threat, so much so that wide roads, beaches, parks, commons and other large open spaces were obstructed by wires, wooden poles, old vehicles and sewer pipes. Lakes, rivers and reservoirs were also attended to: in 1940, Luftwaffe seaplanes had used them as convenient points from which to off-load troops in the seizure of Rotterdam's bridges.

Anti-aircraft weaponry

The devastating, pinpoint attacks by the Junkers Ju 87 Stuka in the campaigns in western Europe in 1940 had brought home the need for the defence of vulnerable sites, such as wireless or power stations, by light anti-aircraft (LAA) weapons. Britain did not possess an adequate number of LAA guns before the war: attempts to purchase Breda 20mm guns from Italy came to nought in 1940 when Italy entered the war on Germany's side. Britain started the war with only 100 of the excellent Swedish 40mm Bofors guns, and prior to the delivery of more of these, to make up for the losses at Dunkirk at least, the obsolete Lewis rifle-calibre

Different designs of pillbox and defence posts could be found on RAF airfields. This is one of a group of three Oakington pillboxes (named after RAF Oakington where they were first designed and used). Each mounted a machine gun and the group created a strongly defended locality at Long Marston airfield in Warwickshire.

machine gun had to be relied on. The only 20mm gun available in any numbers was the RAF's Hispano Suiza aircraft cannon and many of these, when sufficient quantities were available, were placed on improvised mountings to protect airfields and aircraft factories.

Fortunately, the situation concerning heavy anti-aircraft (HAA) weaponry was somewhat more positive. In the summer of 1940 Britain had 1,200 HAA guns organised into seven AA divisions: this would eventually increase to 12. She also possessed an excellent weapon in the 3.7in. AA gun, together with numbers of the 4.5in. gun, and later in the war the 5.25in. turretted naval gun, although at the beginning of the war World War I-era lorry-mounted 3in. guns were still in use for mobile protection. In the event of an invasion the 3.7in. guns would have been used in an AT role, like the German 88mm Flak gun. AA guns were provided with suitable ammunition for the AT role so that they could form additional defended localities. The HAA guns were assisted by barrage balloons, tethered over vulnerable points such as cities, to force enemy bombers higher and therefore limit their bombing accuracy. Whilst the gun barrages improved the morale of the populace, the accuracy of their nightime firing was questionable until the introduction later of radar-controlled guns and proximity fuses.

The HAA sites were manned by members of the Royal Artillery or the Home Guard. There was always a struggle to retain men in AA Command, and so during the course of the war large numbers of the women's ATS were drafted onto HAA sites to operate optical and other equipment, although they were not involved in the loading or firing of the guns. These mixed batteries required the War Office to provide rather more congenial accommodation than the male troops had known. The Home Guard would also assist on many AA batteries, both gun and 'Z' rocket projectile sites. The latter was a Navy-designed weapon, officially known as the 'UP' or 'unrotated projectile' (meaning that the barrel from which it was fired was not rifled). It relied on a high volume of fire rather than accuracy to bring down enemy planes. The rockets were fired from single, double, and nine- and twenty-barrelled projectors. 64 projectors constituted a battery for the single and double versions, whilst 12 constituted a battery for the nine-barrel version. The 20-barrel version constituted a battery in its own right.

Maunsell sea forts

The weakness of existing coast and air defences protecting the Thames and Mersey estuaries had been exploited by the Germans early in the war: bombers approaching from the seaward side met relatively light and restricted HAA. At the request of the Admiralty, the distinguished engineer Guy Maunsell put forward a proposal for the construction of AA forts located in the sea to protect the estuaries. The first of the Navy forts, each equipped with radar, searchlights, 3.7in. HAA and Bofors 40mm LAA guns, was sunk into position in the Thames estuary on 11 February 1942. The inclusion of radar on the forts provided an early warning capability. The last of the four Navy forts built to protect the Thames estuary was sunk into position on 1 August 1942. By this

Although taken over a year after the end of the war, this RAF photograph of Long Newnton airfield, Wiltshire, still shows a wartime landscape. The technical buildings (such as the hangars) remain, as do the dispersed accommodation buildings. The Bristol outer defence line AT ditch can be made out, zig-zagging down from the top left of the photograph. On the original print pillboxes can be seen at the angles of the ditch. The straight line of the Roman Fosse Way runs diagonally across the photograph. (EH)

time Luftwaffe activity was diminishing. The next batch of Maunsell forts to be built under the direction of the Navy was for the defence of the Mersey estuary: these would be sited closer to land than the Navy Thames forts, and would be under the control of the Army. The Army required the AA guns to be spaced 100 yards apart and so a different design was required: each fort comprised seven separate structures, each part having a separate role or dedicated armament. Three further Army forts were built in the Thames estuary. These proved their worth in the V1 offensive, shooting down 30 missiles but also acting as an advanced radar post to warn of the approach of these weapons. The Mersey forts never fired a shot in anger and were dismantled after the war, but a number of the Thames forts survive. In the 1960s their living accommodation was used, in at least one case, to house a 'pirate' radio station.

The ROC

From lonely hilltops, headlands and even derelict windmills the 40,000 volunteer men and women of the Royal Observer Corps (ROC) provided the eyes and ears of the RAF. Around the country were 1,500 open posts constantly manned in all weather by two observers. Details of the identification, height, speed and direction of all aircraft seen or heard were plotted. Whilst their main aim was to locate the movement of enemy aircraft, they were invaluable, too, in plotting allied aircraft that had got into difficulties. The information was relayed via a countrywide telephone network to the ROC control centres, then onto the ADGB organisation who would alert ground and air defences: if an air raid was anticipated, the air raid sirens would be sounded. Although the coastal Chain Home system of early-warning radar had come into use before the war, at the time of the Battle of Britain the Royal Observer Corps was the only means of tracking enemy aircraft around the country once they had crossed the coast. They would also prove of value in the fight against the V1 late in the war. Perhaps the Corps' most famous act was plotting the Deputy Führer Rudolph Hess's aircraft from its crossing of the British coast to its eventual crash-landing in Scotland in May 1941.

The Blitz 1940–41

The Luftwaffe's failure to win mastery of the skies during the Battle of Britain led to a switch in tactics: bombing would now be carried out under cover of darkness. While bombing accuracy might suffer, it would certainly cause terror, injury and death among the civilian population in particular. No longer would bombing be against defined military targets. On moonlit nights, rivers, reservoirs and coastal features would give guidance: there was little that could be done to disguise these.

When conditions were less favourable, the Luftwaffe made use of navigational systems such as the *Knickebein* ('dog's leg'), X-Apparatus (*X-Geräte*), and Y-Apparatus (*Y-Geräte*) systems. They used a sequence of intersecting beams and precision timing devices that guided the bombers to their targets. The British developed jamming techniques to try to counter this. The most

The Chain Home radar system

The Chain Home (CH) radar system played a vital role in the air defence of Great Britain, particularly in the Battle of Britain in 1940. It allowed the early detection of approaching German bombers, and the scrambling of British fighters to counter them, as well as providing advance warning to the civilian population of imminent air raids. The first CH station was at Bawdsey Manor in Suffolk, which was handed over to the RAF in 1937. Towards the end of the war, the stations were also vital in plotting the approach of V rockets, as well as guiding Allied bombers to the launch sites of these weapons. The CH system operated by illuminating an area of sky using an energy pulse, which was then reflected back by any objects encountered. The skill of the listener at the receiving station, coupled with information on friendly aircraft activity in the area, determined whether this object was a threat or not. Most of the CH stations were located along the east and south-east coastline of the UK, and featured huge transmitter towers, making them a key feature of the local landscape. Additional systems were added throughout 1943 (Chain Home Low and Extra Low) to combat the threat of low-flying German bombers, that had learned to avoid radar detection this way. The Chain Home system was gradually run down in the later stages of the war, as the threat of German bombing raids receded, and was replaced by more modern radar technology in the 1950s.

OPPOSITE **5.25in. HAA battery, London, 1943**
This battery, located on Primrose Hill in North London, was one of only three twin-5.25in. HAA emplacements in Britain. These guns were diverted from Navy contracts and were obtained in an exchange for Bofors LAA guns. By the time they became operational in 1943, however, the threat from the Luftwaffe had greatly diminished. The 5.25in. gun (A) has a power plant next to it (B), and camouflage nets to disguise its concrete base (C). To the left of the main gun is a concrete holdfast (D) for a 3.7in.

HAA gun, one of the earlier guns on the site, covered by a camouflage screen. In the battery Command Post (E), ATS personnel would operate the heightfinder (F), spotting binoculars (G), and the predictor (H). An inset (I) shows the layout of a 1941-pattern HAA command post, different to the CP in the main illustration: key features include a Lewis gun (i), heightfinder (ii), predictor (iii), plotting room (iv) and emergency exits (v). A further inset (J) shows the location of the overall site, looking down on London.

An animated scene in the command post of a mixed 3.7in. HAA battery, August 1943. ATS personnel man the predictor in the foreground: this controlled the shell fuse settings and the range, bearing and elevation of the guns. In the centre spotting binoculars are being used, whilst the range finder is being studied in the background. In the upper left-hand corner is one of the guns: the number 5 on the gun pit may indicate that this was a six-gun battery instead of the more usual four guns. (IWM H 32338)

infamous use of these devices was on the night of 13/14 November 1940, when the centre of Coventry was devastated.

The Blitz, as the Luftwaffe offensive came to be known, began in mid-August 1940 and would come to an end only when the Luftwaffe bomber units turned their attention eastwards for the invasion of Russia in June 1941. The great cities of London, Bristol, Liverpool, Southampton, Plymouth, Glasgow, Manchester and others would be subjected to the raiders' incendiary and high-explosive bombs.

Decoys and dummy lights

To give an added measure of protection against enemy bombers, bombing decoys were introduced under the aegis of the RAF's No. 80 Wing. Also known as the 'Beambenders', they were principally responsible for the electronic countermeasures against the Luftwaffe's *X-Geräte* and *Knickebein* bomber navigation systems. Using the facilities of the Shepperton Film Studios and led by Col. Turner, the earliest decoys were designed to lure Luftwaffe day bombers away from genuine targets. False aircraft factories and airfields, complete with false aircraft, were erected. This experiment was not successful and in any event the Luftwaffe soon switched to night-bombing. The earliest night-bombing decoys, aimed at protecting the major cities, were codenamed 'Starfish' and attempted to simulate the different types of fire produced by a bombing raid, the object being to make these the target. A little later came the 'QL' (lighting effect) and 'QF' (fire effect) decoys, which simulated the nighttime appearance, under blackout conditions, of important targets. One example of a QL decoy was 'loco glow', which simulated the dim light given off by the fireboxes of locomotives in a station or marshalling yard. It is still unclear whether the effort put into decoys was worthwhile. Most airfields were further protected by replicating their night landing-light systems some distance away from the airfield, thus hoping to confuse the enemy bombers.

In early 1943 the decision was taken to abandon many of the bombing decoys that had proliferated in remote country areas. Bombing attacks were by now less frequent in many parts of the country, and the land taken up by the decoys could now be used for food production. The men who had run the decoy sites could also be employed in other duties. Many would, no doubt, be pleased that their isolated and somewhat boring service might be replaced by something more stimulating.

Shelter from the bombs

The development and fear of mass bombing led in the late 1930s to the search for bombproof premises for vital commands and departments. The first such site was the Cabinet War Rooms, built before the war, and situated in a reinforced basement beneath offices in Whitehall, London. At the beginning of the war the Admiralty Citadel was built not far from the Cabinet War Rooms in London, to protect the Navy staffs. The German tactic of attempting to destroy the apparatus of government dictated the building of yet more war rooms in inner and outer London. The height of its buildings and the breadth of the River Thames made the centre of London easy to identify from above, and therefore vulnerable to both bomber and surprise parachute attack. Alternative Cabinet War Rooms, known by the code name of 'Paddock', were therefore instituted in the London suburbs at Dollis Hill.

The need for protective shelters also led to the siting in underground quarries and tunnels of bomb and ammunition stores, as well as key national treasures. It also led to the creation of tunnelled shadow factories, such as the Rover car company facility at Drakelow in Worcestershire, which produced engine components for the Bristol aircraft company. A number of Army Commands had specially built underground Battle HQs, such as the one for Western Command in Chester, whilst other commands relied on a system of dispersed facilities. The headquarters of Western Approaches, which controlled and protected the convoys on the Atlantic passage between the United States and Britain, was moved from Plymouth to Liverpool in early 1941, and utilised the basement of a substantial building in the centre of the city as a gas-proof and bomb-proof headquarters.

The Baedeker raids, 1942

Between April and June 1942 the Luftwaffe launched the *Baedeker* raids, named after a famous series of German tourist guides. These raids hit historic and lightly defended cities such as Exeter, Bath and Canterbury and were a reprisal for the RAF's raids on German historic cities. Hitler was apparently so incensed by the RAF's raids that he used the *Baedeker* guidebooks to seek out Britain's most suitable cities for retaliation.

The following figures provide the context for the importance of Britain's air defences during the war. During the course of the Blitz, 43,000 civilians were killed: a further 17,000 were killed in the later *Baedeker* raids, the 'Little Blitz' and in V-weapon attacks. In London a high proportion of the city's housing stock was hit and overall a fifth of the country's housing stock would suffer damage. In addition, the raids had a disturbing effect on the ability of the country's citizens and cities to carry on. Until well into the war civilian casualties from bombing would outstrip military casualties. The men and women who manned Britain's air defences, and the development of technology to give advance warning of raids, were vital to the defence of the nation.

The need for bombproof accommodation led to the construction of specially protected and, in this case, defensible headquarters. This is the Admiralty Citadel in London. In the basement was the vital Operational Intelligence Centre, which fed 'Ultra' intelligence information to HQ Western Approaches during the Battle of the Atlantic.

LAA Bofors position, Hastings, Sussex, 1942

The 40mm Bofors LAA gun, manufactured in Britain but designed in Sweden, was one of the most successful weapons in its class. The gun was used to defend targets from dive-bombers and low-level attack, and many were emplaced along the south coast of England from 1942 onwards to ward off 'tip and run' raiders. In 1944, they also played a key role against the V1 menace. Here a Bofors gun, sited near the Norman castle at Hastings, engages a brace of Focke-Wulf FW 190 fighter-bombers.

The enemy within

Much publicity had been given to the danger from the enemy within. Exaggerated reports from Holland of German paratroops dressed as nuns led to the grossly inflated fear of fifth columnists. (This phrase originated from the Spanish Civil War when, in 1936, the Nationalist Gen. Mola claimed he possessed, in addition to his four columns advancing on Madrid, an extra column. This was composed of the elements within the city that, he believed, would rise and fight for him). Nevertheless, the 'Brandenburg' Regiment did dress as Dutch soldiers to seize a key bridge in Holland in 1940 and they also received help from Dutch Nazi party members. Sensational reports in British newspapers in 1940 suggested that a fifth column already existed in the UK in the form of Fascist sympathisers, communists and foreign aliens already in the country. This fear led to the largely unjustified rounding up of aliens, many of whom were refugees from Nazi persecution, and their evacuation to Canada or the Isle of Man. As the war progressed, the restrictions on aliens were gradually eased and many were later released, some to serve in the armed forces.

The Defence Regulations of 1939 reflected the fear of the 'enemy within'. Any possible method of communicating with the enemy had to be controlled; even racing and homing pigeons were considered to be a threat and authorisation under Regulation 9 (2) had to be obtained from the police for their possession.

Intelligence gathering

The possibility that the 'enemy within' might, by the use of secret radios, be communicating with Germany led, at the beginning of the war, to the setting up of the Radio Security Service manned by civilian members of the Radio Society of Great Britain. Each operator, equipped with a radio, searched the airwaves on a given frequency. Whilst no messages from agents were detected (these having been either arrested or 'turned'), the operation did provide much useful information on enemy signals traffic and led to the significant enlargement of the 'Y' intercept service. The latter, first established in the early 1920s, became part of SIS (Secret Intelligence Service) prior to the war: it provided technical analysis on wireless signals and made a crucial contribution to the overall intelligence effort.

The war witnessed the rapid development of intelligence gathering systems and a series of listening posts ('Y' stations) were built throughout the country to feed intercepted enemy signals traffic to the Government Code and Cipher School (later GCHQ) at Bletchley Park (Station 'X'). The BBC 'Y' station, for example, at Woodnorton in Worcestershire, reported a daily digest of all received transmissions to the Government. The RAF 'Y' station at Cheadle in Staffordshire intercepted and decrypted low grade Luftwaffe signals traffic and could anticipate bombing raids,

The Home Guard carries out a training exercise with 'Germans' in Shropshire 1943. In the absence of jackboots, the 'Germans' wear rubber Wellington boots, but otherwise look realistic. The corporal has a Sten gun, by then the standard weapon for NCOs. (IWM H 30176)

this information being passed directly to the ADGB organisation. Other organisations would also be involved in the 'wireless war', one of the most controversial being the Special Operations Executive (SOE) whose agents (both male and female) were trained in parachuting and the techniques of unarmed combat and sabotage in secret locations around the country. To keep in touch with their agents on operations overseas SOE had wireless stations in Oxfordshire at Thame, Grendon Underwood and Henley.

Code breaking at Bletchley Park

The rapid expansion of the 'wireless war' led to the search for men and women with the ability to break enemy codes. Those at Bletchley Park were recruited from universities and museums. The pressure on the workers there was such that nervous breakdowns were all too frequent. The 'Ultra' information, as the code breaking came to be known, was received from a network of 'Y' intercept stations manned by Navy, RAF, and Army personnel and also by a number of civilians. It helped significantly in many spheres of the war, especially in winning the Battle of the Atlantic.

Guerrilla warfare and covert groups

The concept of guerrilla warfare had, rather surprisingly, been granted attention in the conservative circles of the War Office in the 1930s. A small team of officers had studied the subject and had prepared a number of pamphlets, which, they thought, might be of value to potential resistance movements in a future war. The leading figure in this small circle was Maj. Colin Gubbins who would head the British resistance movement at the beginning of the war and, later, the SOE. The latter carried the idea of resistance warfare to the occupied countries, to 'set Europe ablaze'.

The likelihood of invasion in the summer of 1940 led to the establishment of two parallel organisations: the Auxiliary Units and the Special Duties Section. The former would be involved in acts of sabotage behind the invader's lines whilst the latter would be an intelligence-gathering organisation, communicating information about German forces in their areas by specially designed radio sets. So important was this organisation that, with Churchill's backing, it ranked in priority above the Regular Army: the Auxiliary Units were the first to receive the new Plastic Explosive. They were primarily situated in the coastal counties in the south and east of the country, but were also to be found in South Wales and, to protect the vital area of the Midlands, in Herefordshire and Worcestershire.

Operating nocturnally from carefully camouflaged underground bases, the small teams were tasked with creating disorder and carrying out acts of sabotage in the enemy's rear areas. It was realised that the life span of each team, or Patrol as they were known, would be no more than a couple of weeks. After D-Day in June 1944, many Patrols, thanks to their training in night operations, were sent to guard installations on the south coast against possible enemy raids whilst others provided nightime protection for the Royal family. A number of the Auxiliers would also find their way into SOE or the SAS, where their skills were much appreciated. Nominally a member of the Home Guard, the Auxilier wore uniform.

The members of the ultra-secret Auxiliary Units were recruited from men, often very young men, who could find their way around their country areas at night and could live off the land if necessary. The farming community, whose eldest sons were in a reserved occupation, provided perhaps the largest pool of volunteers. One farmer's son, Geoffrey Morgan-Jones from Herefordshire, was told that their job was to be 'a bloody nuisance to Jerry'. Others such as senior scouts and gamekeepers were picked, and even known poachers were considered. The Patrol sergeants were local, respected men and each county was under the control of an Intelligence Officer. Perhaps the best known of these was Peter Fleming, brother of the novelist Ian Fleming, who established patrols in Kent in 1940. It was vital that the men were fit, if only to survive the rigours of the unarmed combat training they received: a revolutionary concept at the time, it would, in future, become standard military training.

In contrast to the Auxiliers, the members of the shadowy Special Duties Section (SDS), controlled by a Maj. Petherick MP from Coleshill House in Wiltshire, which was also the

Despatch riders of HQ Wing 2nd Battalion Wiltshire Home Guard are ready for action in the town of Malmesbury, Wiltshire. The author's father-in-law, Fred Sharpe, is second from the left.

HQ of the Auxiliary Units, did not wear a formal uniform. Set up as independent cells, the civilian spies would have put messages into dead letter drops to be collected by young messengers for delivery to the radio operator. This person would often be a prominent figure in the community such as a doctor or vicar and who would have a legitimate reason for moving amongst his community. The messages were passed to Corps of Signals underground 'Zero Stations' where they would be passed onto Command HQs. Another source of reconnaissance and signals would be provided by the covert organisation called 'Phantom', born out of the chaos of the Battle of France, which would conduct reconnaissance around the battle area and report conditions back to GHQ by wireless. They would later be used to good effect in the fighting in Europe after D-Day.

The men and women of the SDS were controlled by a local Intelligence Officer, again a respected individual. They were forced to adhere to the Official Secrets Act, and conformed to a code of absolute secrecy, two factors which mean that we know very little about the SDS today. Many of the hundreds if not thousands of volunteers maintained their secrets to the grave; an impressive testament. Only recently have the small number of survivors felt able to tell their stories.

A number of women Home Guard Auxiliaries were trained in the use of radio sets later in the war with a view to their carrying out a communications role, but they were not armed. These ladies are with a detachment of the Kidderminster Home Guard: their 'uniform' consisted only of a Home Guard Auxiliary metal badge and an armband.

The invasion threat recedes

The failure of the Luftwaffe in the first phase of the Battle of Britain, which lasted from mid-June to mid-September 1940, meant that the strategically vital 'aerial artillery' provided by the level-bombers and the accurate but slow and vulnerable Junkers Ju 87 Stuka dive-bomber, could not have operated with impunity during the projected invasion. A key factor in the RAF's victory was that it was now aided by the revolutionary radar early-warning stations, of which the Luftwaffe was initially ignorant.

The decision by Hitler in September 1940, following RAF attacks on Berlin, to switch his bombers from attacking RAF airfields to bombing London further affected the invasion preparations. The Italian Navy, which Hitler in Directive No.16 had hoped would tie down the Royal Navy in the Mediterranean, was equally frustrated: the aerial attack by the Fleet Air Arm in November 1940 on the Italian fleet at Taranto meant that it would be of no use to the Axis cause for many months. Conversely, more British naval reserves could therefore be allocated to possible anti-invasion measures. Additionally, Mussolini's offer of troops for SEALION was disdainfully refused by Hitler, although bombers of the Regia Aeronautica would appear briefly and ineffectually over eastern England in November 1940.

Hitler's order that all preparations be in place by mid-August 1940 was impractical: the Kriegsmarine was just not ready. It was inferior in size to the Royal Navy and had already suffered heavy losses in the Norwegian campaign. The invasion barges and shipping, gathering in Dutch, Belgian and northern French ports, had been photographed by PRU (Photographic Reconnaissance Unit) Supermarine Spitfires and had been bombed by the RAF. Nor was the Kriegsmarine particularly enthusiastic about the operation itself. Even if the first wave gained a footing it might be several weeks before weather conditions were favourable to transport the second, third and fourth waves plus the re-supplies. So much depended on the weather and tidal conditions. And so the August deadline for the invasion of Britain slipped by. Those vessels that had not been destroyed by RAF bombing gradually returned to their pre-Operation SEALION locations as, with the onset of winter, the window of opportunity had now closed, at least for 1940. In any event, Hitler, who had had an equivocal enthusiasm for the seaborne invasion of Britain, now turned to another and more momentous operation: BARBAROSSA, the invasion and destruction of his ideological enemy the Soviet Union, planned for May 1941; something, he claimed, that would make the world hold its breath. Whilst SEALION was left in place as a potential threat to Britain, the movement of the launch month for BARBAROSSA from May to June meant that launching SEALION in late-summer 1941 was less likely. Germany's failure to deliver the Soviet Union a fatal blow that year further diminished the likelihood of invasion. The entry of the United States of America into the war at the end of 1941 and the arrival of US forces and equipment in the UK from 1942 onwards put paid to any further German invasion plans.

The Auxiliary Units and Special Duties Section were ultra-secret stay-behind organisations. The latter would have acted as spies and had wireless sets to communicate with Army signals sections. The Auxiliary Units were tasked with sabotage. 'Adam' Patrol, located to the west of Hereford, is shown here in 1944.

A nation at war

For the civilian, the first clouds of war appeared with the passing of the Air Raid Precautions Act of 1937. It was anticipated that in addition to high-explosive and incendiary bombs, the enemy would use air-delivered poison gas. The Italians had used gas in Abyssinia and many men had first-hand experience of poison gas warfare in World War I. This led to the introduction of gas masks for all well before the outbreak of war. Other measures included the painting of postbox tops with yellowish-green gas detector paint, together with the issue of instructions on how to make the home gas proof.

The Civil Defence movement

The evolution of the Civil Defence services (an umbrella organisation comprising air-raid wardens, observers and rescue services, and the like) was slow and it was left to local councils, with central government aid, to initiate civil defence measures. The country was split into several regions, each one having a Regional Commissioner. A whole raft of services had to be introduced, or existing services co-ordinated, to cope with the anticipated casualties and damage resulting from bombing raids. Such services included: first aid posts, gas decontamination stations, hospitals, demolition and repair squads, Police, the Auxiliary Ambulance Service, Fire Guards, Air Raid Wardens, Control and Report Stations, despatch riders, reserve firemen, and light and heavy rescue squads.

The protection of the civilian population had to be addressed, which led to the countrywide introduction of air-raid shelters. For domestic protection the Anderson Shelter (named after Sir John Anderson, the Home Secretary) was introduced. It was free to those on limited incomes: one drawback though was

If the Invader Comes was issued by the British Government in June 1940, in response to the threat of invasion, giving instructions to the population on how to behave in the event. The closing words are: 'Think before you act. But think always of your country before you think of yourself'.
Beating the Invader was issued somewhat later than *If the Invader Comes*, in May 1941, in response to the renewed threat of invasion. Its message was typically Churchillian, ending with the advice: 'Do not tell the enemy anything. Do not give him anything. Do not help him in any way'. Hitler's invasion of Russia a month later made the instruction redundant.

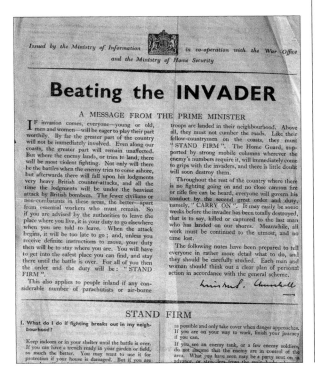

A family spends a winter night in their living room, which has been fitted with struts to form an integral air raid shelter. The father is a police Special Constable, and his helmet and gas mask hang with the others. (RF)

The war was not without its lighter moments. The enforcement of the blackout regulations ('Put that light out') was carried out by Air Raid Wardens (the author's father was one), who often had a reputation for being overly keen. (BPC)

that many houses did not have gardens into which they could be sunk. The Morrison shelter (named after Herbert Morrison, the Minister of Home Security), introduced in late-1941 for indoor use, resolved this problem. Schools were provided with trench or surface shelters, and in town centres basements were reinforced to accommodate those who might be caught during daylight raids. However, many families preferred to stay in their own homes rather than use the unwholesome public shelters, and it was only due to public pressure that the deep stations of the London Underground system were made available. Here, again, the question of public hygiene and privacy was given little attention.

To prevent Luftwaffe aircraft identifying urban centres, blackout regulations were introduced at the start of the war. Cars were only permitted one masked headlamp and public and other lighting was eliminated or vastly reduced. Thick blackout curtains had to be fitted across windows too. The police rigorously enforced any breaches of the regulations. The situation did not ease until the end of 1944 by which time a great increase in serious accidents to motorists and pedestrians had taken place. Roadside obstructions, including trees, were painted with white bands to prevent pedestrians and drivers running into them under blackout conditions, and white lines were painted down roads and along kerbs.

The first Blitz raid in September 1940 highlighted many defects, especially in the operation of the fire brigades. Until the Fire Brigade Act of 1938 there was no legal requirement for local authorities to provide a fire brigade: as a result of the Act they were now under a duty to so. Professional firemen trained the part-time volunteers of the Auxiliary Fire Service, which had been created in 1938 in anticipation of war. However, different authorities used different types of equipment and the hoses of one brigade did not necessarily fit the hydrants in an adjoining local authority. It was also difficult to mobilise such a disparate organisation in the event of a major air raid. To correct this, in early 1941, a National Fire Service was established that came under central government control and featured a commonality of equipment. Other Civil Defence services made do with ad hoc vehicles including requisitioned taxis towing water pumps, whilst the ambulance services used hastily converted commercial vehicles such as bread vans. This amateurish approach was made to work by the steadfastness and selfless behaviour of the volunteers.

Evacuation

The belief that major cities would sustain horrific casualties once the enemy's bombing campaign commenced led to the meticulous pre-war planning of evacuation procedures. Beginning on 1 September 1939, in a period of only three days, 1.5 million women and children were sent from the cities into the countryside to avoid the expected holocaust. The migration took place by train, and went extremely smoothly; however, there were no systems in place to cope with their arrival in the countryside. A social shock lay in wait for many country dwellers who accommodated slum children and their parents. The alien environment in the countryside led to many mothers and children drifting back into the cities, especially when the anticipated bombing did not occur. Even during the height of the 1940 Blitz many preferred to stay put in the cities as family units and to accept the risks.

The National Service Bill, 1941

In late-1941 the National Service Bill was introduced: working men could now be conscripted into the part-time Civil Defence and Home Guard. The two organisations were therefore able to fill the gaps caused by the call-up of men into the forces, and also to dispose of those considered less suitable for such work due to their age or infirmity. However, many of those who had originally volunteered in 1940 felt that this was a step backwards, as some of the conscripted men did not always show the same levels of commitment. The Bill also introduced important changes for women: now unmarried women between 20 and 30 years of age could be called up for service in the new ordnance factories, into the Land Army or into military service. In the latter case, with the creation of mixed HAA batteries, this could mean exposure to enemy fire. A majority, however, were allowed to opt for service in civilian occupations rather than the armed forces.

The pre-war Women's Voluntary Service (WVS), later awarded royal patronage for its war work to become the Women's Royal Voluntary Service, provided many essential services. Its members, before the full establishment of the Home Guard, played their part in the summer of 1940 by manning the observation posts watching out for airborne invasion. When pressure was brought to bear for women to be allowed to join the Home Guard, the initial response was that the WVS was already providing an adequate support service: however, women would later serve in small numbers in the Home Guard as clerical auxiliaries or wireless operators. They also formed part of the Civil Defence system by providing food for bombed-out families and refreshments for rescue squads. Their members were also busy, for example, in the garnishing of camouflage nets for the Army and in organising the collection of rose hips as a vitamin C substitute. Other voluntary groups 'doing their bit' included the Salvation Army, the Red Cross and St John's Ambulance Brigade.

One area of work not considered suitable for women was coal mining. The conscription of large numbers of young men from the traditional coal mining areas put a great strain on the older men left working the pits, many of whom were often in poor health. Productivity in the deep mines actually fell throughout the war, at a time when demand was very high. The opening up of open cast sites was only a partial corrective. At the end of 1943, to alleviate the problem, one in ten young men were conscripted for National Service and were compulsorily sent to the coal mines. These would be known as 'Bevin Boys', a name taken from the then Minister of Labour, Ernest Bevin. Whilst it may have broadened the minds of those sent to the pits, it probably did little to help the overall situation.

The protection of Britain's economy

Britain depended for much of its food on imports. The swingeing losses of shipping and cargoes in the Battle of the Atlantic between 1939 and 1943 were somewhat offset by attempts to make the country more self sufficient in food. Less meat would be produced and much of the country's pastureland would be turned over to the production of crops. War Agricultural Committees, with draconian powers, controlled food production. At the same time cold and grain stores were built to ensure that there were reserves of food available away from vulnerable ports. Land that had hitherto been unproductive was ploughed with the new agricultural machinery imported from America under the Lend-Lease system and enriched with newly invented fertilisers. Householders were encouraged to grow food in the little free time they possessed, and to 'Dig for Victory'. Food scraps were collected to feed the pigs that produced bacon, rationed like many other foodstuffs.

The population and the invasion

Whilst the military aspects of the anticipated invasion exercised the military mind, the question of what to do with the civilian population caught up in fighting had to be considered too. Many people were evacuated from the towns and cities of the coastal counties most at risk from invasion, but the civilians living in the more rural areas would be left to fend for themselves. The Government did not want a repetition of the experiences in France where fleeing refugees clogged the main roads blocking military traffic, and so instructions were issued for the population to 'stay put'. Had there been an invasion it is likely that civilian casualties would have been very heavy. To reinforce the need for the civilian population to stay where they were, as well as giving general advice on invasion issues, a number of leaflets were issued to householders. Among these were 'If the Invader Comes', 'Beating the Invader' and 'Stay Where You Are'. To give reassurance and protection to the towns and cities likely to be targeted first, Invasion Committees were established under the aegis of the Ministry of Home Security. More resources for civil defence were allocated to those centres of communication that would be bombed as part of the enemy 'softening-up' process. Should particularly important areas come under attack, adequate food, water, shelter, sanitation and first aid facilities would be made available to support the population during any investment.

The morning after an air raid, May 1941

A family emerges from their corrugated steel Anderson shelter after a bombing raid. The shelter is semi-sunken within their garden and mounded over with earth for extra protection. The 'spirit of the Blitz' is belied by the fact that the family also took their cash box into the shelter: petty crime continued even during such raids. Behind them, their neighbours have not been so fortunate, as witnessed by the rubble of their home. Civil Defence workers are helping the injured and a food van has arrived.

WILLS'S CIGARETTES

MEDIUM TRAILER FIRE-PUMP

WILLS'S CIGARETTES

AIR RAID WARDENS AND CIVILIAN VOLUNTEER DESPATCH-RIDER

WILLS'S CIGARETTES

THE CIVILIAN RESPIRATOR

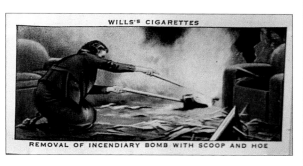

WILLS'S CIGARETTES

REMOVAL OF INCENDIARY BOMB WITH SCOOP AND HOE

To cope with all this increased agricultural activity and to replace male agricultural workers who had been conscripted into the forces, the Women's Land Army (WLA) was revived. It had been set up in World War I to channel young women into working the land, and in World War II was led by Lady Denman until her resignation in 1945. Her resignation was prompted by the poor treatment of the WLA at stand down (they received no demobilisation grants for their hard work and were only able to retain a part of their allotted clothing). There was also a Women's Timber Corps whose members took on the heavy work of forestry – not that the WLA's 80,000 members had an easier time of it, with long hours, harsh weather, difficult employers and inadequate clothing. Whilst the wartime summers were warm and dry, the winters were hard and the women had to take this in their stride. Many would take to life on the land and marry into farming families where their experience and training was prized.

The war economy: defensive growth
In 1939 the military occupied a quarter of a million acres of land: by 1944 this figure had risen to 11.5 million acres, 20 per cent of the total UK land. A large influx of Irish labour took place to build the new airfields, roads and camps, brought about by the lack of British manpower. Existing airfields were extended, and hundreds of new ones built, to occupy in total 360,000 acres of land. Airfields were required for the fighters and bombers taking the fight to the enemy, leading eventually to the RAF's devastating thousand-bomber raids, when the skies over East Anglia were filled with aircraft. The Navy required new harbours and facilities for munitions storage as well as airfields for the Fleet Air Arm. Such were the conflicting demands for agricultural land and suitable flat land for airfields that some airfields were sited in poor locations, for example in parts of the country prone to fog. There was a massive increase in railway activity to cope with the movement of troops, supplies, coal, steel and food to and from ports, and the many civilians being transported to new places and types of work. During periods of blackout the passenger carriages were illuminated by blue light bulbs. Branch lines were built to connect new factories to the main network, extra signal boxes of a wartime ARP (Air Raid Precautions) design were built, and previously redundant lines were reopened.

Before the war, preparations were already in hand to protect the civilian population against air raids. These cigarette cards are from a set advising on protection against gas and incendiary attack. (IT)

One of the bombproof tunnels of the Rover company at Drakelow, Worcestershire. The company produced aircraft engine components for the Bristol aircraft company. During the Cold War the tunnels were assigned to housing a Regional Seat of Government.

In fact freight movement increased by a third over pre-war figures. The railways also carried the few luxury goods still being produced for export to earn vital dollars, such as fine china and whisky.

There were other effects on the country too. By-passes built before the war to cope with increased traffic were closed and used to store military motor transport. The wooded parkland of large country houses was also used for this purpose, and the houses themselves were often used as the headquarters of RAF Groups and other military HQs. Much of the countryside not suitable for cultivation was taken over for military use, such as the training of tank crews or as gunnery and bombing ranges. Commando and Arctic warfare training was conducted in the wild countryside of the Scottish Highlands whilst Snowdonia was used for mountain warfare training. In the New Forest the estate houses of Lord Beaulieu were used for the instruction of SOE operatives. In the same forest at Ashley Walk the RAF tested special munitions such as the giant 'Grand Slam' 22,000lb bomb and the 'Upkeep' bouncing bomb. In the area a structure was built to simulate a U-boat pen roof and different types of bomb were tested on the pen. Members of the RAF's 617 'Dam Busters' Squadron trained on the Derwent reservoirs in the Derbyshire Peak District. Tatton Park in Cheshire, the estate of Lord Egerton, served as a convenient dropping zone for paratroopers and SOE agents undergoing training at nearby Ringway Airfield.

Foreign residents swell the defender's ranks

The German occupation of much of Europe saw a massive influx of foreign nationals intending to fight on the side of Britain: if they could not fight on their home soil then Britain would provide a suitable base leading to the eventual and long-awaited invasion of France in June 1944. Others would come from the Commonwealth and Dominions, the US and Eire. Canadian troops would have played a vital role in the defence of the south of England

had invasion taken place. A massive contribution was made by Polish and also Czech pilots during the Battle of Britain. In 1940 and 1941 Polish troops played a vital part in the construction and guarding of the anti-invasion defences of eastern Scotland. The contributions of the men and women from Norway, Belgium, Holland, Denmark, Yugoslavia and Greece were significant, too.

The arrival of US forces from 1942 onwards marked a turning point in the war and the recognition that Britain's darkest days were coming to a close. Over 1.5 million US troops arrived in the country between January 1943 and June 1944. New airfields were constructed or existing RAF ones handed over to the US 8th Army Air Force mainly on the eastern side of the country for the coming bombing campaign against Germany. Fighter bases would also be required to protect the bombers. Other units, such as the 'Carpetbaggers', with their glossy black B-24 Liberator bombers, flew agent-dropping missions over occupied Europe.

A Military Police Traffic Control unit (note the 'T.C.' on the vehicles) carries out exercises in the south of England in September 1940. Noteworthy is the use of requisitioned transport, an expedient adopted by the Army to move reserves and other units in the desperate days of 1940. These are civilian motor coaches still bearing their civilian registration numbers, but with the addition of an overall coat of camouflage paint. (IWM H 3469)

1944–45: Hitler's vengeance weapons

Peenemünde

On 9 November 1943 in a speech at the Mansion House, not far from the Cabinet War Rooms, Churchill warned the country: 'We cannot exclude the possibility of new forms of attack on this island'. Churchill was not merely trying to eradicate any complacency given the infrequency of bombing raids from June 1941 onwards: he had sufficient intelligence from PRU flights over northern France and Germany, 'Ultra' decrypts and agents' reports to know that the enemy would soon have new weapons at his disposal. Flights over the Baltic by Mosquito reconnaissance aircraft had spotted major activity on the coast at Peenemünde in Germany. Missile-like objects had been seen on the ground, and even missile launches witnessed. Intelligence reports revealed the existence of a small pilotless aircraft (the V1, also known to the Germans by its manufacturer's name Fieseler Fi 103), launched from a rail, and a vertically launched rocket (the V2, known also as the A4).

To counter the threat posed by this German research establishment, a heavy bombing raid was launched by RAF Bomber Command on the night of 17/18 August 1943, codenamed Operation CROSSBOW. The aircrews were not told of the true nature of the target site. Almost 600 aircraft took part in the raid, comprising Lancaster, Halifax and Stirling bombers, and some 40 aircraft and their crew were lost during the mission. Numerous workers, scientists and technicians were killed on the ground, including several key figures in the research program: unfortunately a large number of the fatalities were conscript

The sinister form of the pilotless V1 flying bomb. The small nose propeller operated a mechanism that, at a given distance, caused the bomb to fall to earth. This example is at the RAF Aerospace Museum at Cosford, Shropshire.

labourers, who as such were denied access to any form of shelter. Although the mission was only partly successful in terms of the destruction of the site, it did put back development work at Peenemünde by several months.

Defending against the V1

The British nation soon turned its attention to the forthcoming invasion of France: hard standings were built along the south coast of England for the launching of invasion craft. However, at the highest levels of command there was still concern that the enemy's new weapons could disrupt the invasion, despite some initial scepticism as to whether the existence of such weapons was merely propaganda. From the end of 1943 plans were put in place for the defence of London, Portsmouth, Southampton and Bristol against the flying bombs. London would be protected by lines of fighter patrols and a great belt of eight-gun HAA batteries located to the south of the North Downs in Surrey. Barrage balloons would provide a screen around the capital.

Such caution was not misplaced. The V1 missile plan had been in development since 1942, and was already well advanced, with much construction work on launch sites taking place in 1943 and 1944. The parallel development of other, even more deadly threats, the V2 and V3 weapons, was another reason for concern. Once discovered, the launching rails for the Vl and the hardened sites for the V2 missiles in northern France were pounded by the RAF and USAAF. So concerted was this effort that by 6 June 1944 it was believed that the threat had been removed. In fact, in respect of the Vl, the Germans were already adopting new tactics by siting new, easily erected launching rails in centres of population or disguising them using other forms of camouflage. The first Vl to land on London came in the immediate aftermath of D-Day, launched from a site between the River Seine and the Belgian border of France, and landing in Bethnal Green. Thousands more would follow, causing over 6,000 fatalities.

Once launched and on its way to Britain, this small missile, flying at about 3,000ft, posed severe tactical problems to the defenders. It was potentially possible to launch 200–300 per day, a volume that could swamp the resources of the defenders. It flew at a speed of up to 400mph, almost as fast as the then-fastest RAF fighters. Fighter pilots needed to close in on the small target, risking being brought down by the ensuing explosion. As an alternative to cannon fire, a risky tactic adopted was to fly alongside the V1 and attempt to flip it over, upsetting the guidance gyroscope, and causing it to crash. Its operating height and small size presented grave problems to HAA and LAA defences. The pre-D-Day defensive tactics were found to be severely wanting: for example, LAA and HAA could not engage the missiles when they had entered the fighter 'box'.

In July 1944 Gen. Pile, Commander-in-Chief of AA Command was finally given a free hand in the re-organisation of the defences. A massive migration of guns, Nissen huts, troops and their equipment moved in three days to the south coast of England to form a 5,000 yd-deep 'Diver Belt'. This would leave the defence of the rear area to the fighter aircraft. Guns were moved from 'safe' parts of the country and priority was given to the powered version of the 3.7in. gun. New devices, such as the US SCR 584 Ground Controlled Interception radar and the British-invented but US-developed proximity fuse, helped the AA forces to build up an impressive hit rate of up to 75 per cent of V1s destroyed (comprising all means). Allied disinformation also led the Germans to believe that the V1 was overshooting London (many were in fact falling short), leading to the missile's range being further curtailed.

The advance of the Allies in France in 1944 denied the Germans launching sites in the Pas de Calais and the missiles were moved to Dutch sites, whilst others were launched over the sea by Heinkel bomber aircraft. By the time that the last V1 flew, landing in Suffolk on 29 March 1945, some 10,500 had been launched and around 4,000 had been destroyed.

The V1 (Fieseler Fi 103)

The V1 was launched from a metal ramp, using a catapult slingshot to provide its initial momentum, after which its Argus pulse jet engine took over. The sound of the engine was likened to a large motorcycle: the British nicknamed it the 'Doodlebug'. At a designated distance, determined by an air log in the nose of the missile, the V1 went into a shallow dive. On early versions, the engine cut out at the beginning of the dive, giving an audible warning to those on the ground, a defect that was later corrected. The detonation of the 2,000 lb of explosives on board caused massive damage: strict security was imposed in Britain to deny the enemy knowledge of where the missiles had landed. The first V1 launch sites were begun in mid-1943 and several types were built, from complex bunker systems to simple ramps and storage facilities. The latter were important to the launch sites, as items such as fuel and chemicals needed to be readily available. Examples of permanent sites destined for V1 use include the Blockhaus de Siracourt (near Saint-Pol-sur-Ternoise, France) and the Blockhaus de Lottinghem. Logistical support for the supply of such materials was also a key factor in the location of the sites, as road and rail links were vital. Thousands of V1 rockets were launched from hundreds of bases in France.

The next development in German ballistic weaponry was the V2, or Aggregat 4 as it was originally known. It carried a powerful warhead with huge destructive power, and had a range of over 200 miles. Unlike the V1, it launched by its own power, and on a vertical trajectory: it reached maximum speed rapidly, before falling to earth from a great height. During flight the rocket was steered by a series of rudders and vanes. At the appropriate time, the fuel supply would be shut off, causing the rocket to fall to earth. The rocket would hit its target at several times the speed of sound, causing eye-witnesses to see the explosion prior to hearing the final, rapid descent of the weapon – a factor that denied those unfortunate enough to be near by the opportunity of taking cover. The first firing of the V2 was on 8 September 1944, launched against the city of Paris. London was targetted soon afterwards, and would receive another 500 or so hits before war's end. Due to its inaccuracy, the V2 was best suited to hitting extensive target areas, such as large cities. The V2 offensive lasted from September 1944 until March 1945.

The V2

The V2 could be launched from either heavily protected, underground bases, or from difficult to detect mobile centres, particularly those in Germany and Holland late in the war. Between 1943 and 1944, much effort was put into the construction of launch sites for this weapon in France in particular. One such site was the Watten bunker at Éperlecques in France. Development work on this site had begun back in January 1943. Although they were aware of construction work taking place, the British authorities did not know what its purpose was: some thought it to be a new power station. The bunker at Éperlecques was almost complete by mid-1943, and in common with many Organisation Todt projects, it was built by slave labour (see Fortress 3: *U-Boat Bases and Bunkers 1940–45*). The main drawback of the large, permanent bunkers was that they were easy to spot from the air. The Allies were quick to act against the completed site. The Watten bunker at Éperlecques was bombed repeatedly in August 1943, and was hit again in two 'Tallboy' raids on 17 June and 25 July 1944. Watten may have been put out of action, but there were many more bases being prepared to launch the V2, such as La Coupole at Helfaut-Wizernes, near St-Omer.

Following the failed attempt on Hitler's life in mid-1944, the control of the 'V' weapons program passed to the SS. It was not long after, in September 1944, that the first V2 rockets reached their targets, launched from mobile stations beyond the eastern borders of France. These mobile stations were easy to camouflage: although they featured a large number of logistical vehicles, troops and technicians to support, fuel, arm and erect the trailer-carried rocket, they could more easily escape the attention of Allied aircraft than a large concrete structure with its access roads and railway tracks.

The first V2 to land on Britain came down in Chiswick, London on 8 September 1944, having been launched from Holland. Once in the air, there was no defence against this weapon. Only by over-running the launch sites, disrupting the construction and movement of the missiles and the fuels that powered them could they be stopped. The last V2 was launched on 27 March 1945: the 1,115 missiles that landed on Britain caused 2,700 deaths. Despite the extensive construction programmes, no V2 rockets were ever launched from France.

The vast Watten bunker in the forest of Éperlecques in northern France, one of a number under construction from early 1943 for the assembly and launching of V2 rockets against London. The discovery of this and other bunkers by PRU aircraft sealed their fate: RAF 12,000 lb 'Tallboy' and USAAF 'Aphrodite' pilotless converted B17 and B24 flying bombs damaged the sites so badly that work was abandoned before they became operational.

A surviving Allan-Williams turret forming part of the River Severn stop-line at Buildwas, Shropshire. It was designed to revolve and to mount different types of light machine gun and had a secondary LAA role (note the circular hole for this purpose). Shortages of steel restricted the manufacture of this type of defence post.

The V3 (Hochdruckpumpe)

Near the village of Mimoyecques, in the Pas de Calais, France, Hitler ordered the construction of an extensive bunker complex (designed by Albert Speer) that would house and protect his latest 'vengeance' weapon, the V3 gun. This massive, howitzer had been under development since early 1942. It was a multi-chambered, long-range gun, with the capacity to fire its 15cm shells up to a range of just over 100 miles, more than enough to reach London: a rate of fire of 300 shells per hour was predicted, though it is doubtful whether this would have been achievable. The 25 barrels of its guns were each 426.5ft long, and were sunk into long shafts in a hillside. In late-1943 and July 1944, Allied bombers targetted the Mimoyecques bunker, causing extensive damage. The Germans abandoned the site at this point, and it was later sealed up by British Royal Engineers, having been overrun in late-1944. Its massive guns were never fired.

Great ingenuity and effort had been expended on the V weapon programme but it came too late to have any impact on the war. It had failed to disrupt OVERLORD and those missiles that did land were insufficient in number to significantly affect the morale of the Blitz-hardened Londoners. However, the V1 had the distinction of being the first operational 'cruise missile' whilst the V2 would lead directly to the development of space travel in the post-war world. Both were truly revolutionary weapons.

Aftermath

Stand-down of the defences

From the beginning of 1944 onwards, the realisation that the war was moving in the Allies' favour, coupled with the insatiable demand for steel, led to the gradual removal of redundant anti-invasion defences such as mines, barbed wire, beach scaffolding and metal AT and anti-landing obstacles. There had to be a good case for the physical removal of obsolete defence works though, for example, to free-up agricultural land. As an incentive, farmers were offered £5 for each pillbox destroyed on their land. The removal of AT concrete blocks and defence positions was welcomed in particular by the population, as these often impinged upon the highways. Progress was slow as labour was rarely available. Some redundant pillboxes suffered the indignity of being used to train troops in assault and demolition techniques in readiness for D-Day, or as targets for different types of artillery.

The success of the June 1944 Normandy landings added further weight to the argument that the country's defences were rapidly approaching obsolescence. In late-July 1944 the Home Guard was informed that due to the steel shortage all steel AT rails were to be withdrawn. The Royal Engineers' Directorate of Demolition and Recovery would carry out their removal and disposal. Concrete blocks and cylinders were not to be removed, as these would be retained to form roadblocks, which might still be needed, together with any additional obstructions that could be improvised locally. These would be reinforced by the use of the No.75 AT grenade (Hawkins) and the 2pdr AT gun that was now in use by the Home Guard, plus any other available weapons.

In September 1944 a draft memo from GHQ Home Forces to Home Commands stated that there was no need to maintain Home Guard defence works and the tentative suggestion was made that its members should start clearing away barbed wire and other obstructions. It was, however, appreciated that the sheer scale of the country's anti-invasion defences meant that it would take a considerable amount of time to clear them away, something that would present a manpower problem even in the post-war period.

In November 1944 demolition was already underway on the blast walls and pillboxes protecting vital Government offices in London, such as the Air Ministry. This work was carried on here and at other sites through 1945. In February 1946 *War Illustrated* reported on a pillbox undergoing demolition by pneumatic drill at the end of Folkestone Pier, the nearest point to the French coast. The work carried on through 1946 too: mechanical 'navvies' worked

The Cabinet War Rooms, London

The fear of the mass-bombing of British cities lead in the late-1930s to the provision of bomb-proof accommodation for the members of British central government. In June 1938 work began on reinforcing the basement of the Office of Works building in Whitehall, London, the exterior of which is shown in the inset illustration. The building itself was a strong one and it was conveniently situated between the Houses of Parliament and 10 Downing Street, the home of the British Prime Minister. A 3ft-thick concrete and steel 'slab' (1) was installed over the basement of the building, together with a sub-layer of interlocking steel beams (2). The weight of this structure was supported by timber and brick props and pillars in the basement and sub-basement. At the heart of the underground complex lay the Cabinet Room (3): in May 1940 Churchill declared: 'This is the room from which I will direct the war'. During the course of the war over 100 meetings of the War Cabinet were held here. In addition to the main Cabinet Room, other areas contained secretarial offices, canteens, dormitories, Churchill's bedroom and a Map Room. Much of the facility is now open to the public.

through the night to clear the 40-person air-raid shelters from London's Lower Regent Street. When this was completed it provided the first view up to Piccadilly since the early days of the war. In April 1946 air-raid shelters around Nelson's column in Trafalgar Square were also removed in preparation for the great victory parade to be held on 8 June 1946. Outside the capital, many miles of AT ditches were filled in, once again to maximise the availability of agricultural land. The deadly job of removing the thousands of mines sown on beaches and inland fell to the men of the Royal Engineers. There were many tragic deaths caused by beach mines shifting from their original positions.

Debris from demolished shelters and destroyed buildings was ground and crushed, providing a basic construction material for the making of exterior and partition walls in the many new buildings now urgently needed. Civilian housing was a key priority, and so at the beginning of 1945 some 3,000 US combat engineers were put at the disposal of the Government for the clearance of bombsites as well as for the erection of temporary housing. This need also led to aircraft factories switching production at the end of the war to the manufacture of pre-fabricated buildings, known as 'prefabs'. Another vital part of the labour force comprised prisoners of war, many of whom remained in their camps until long after the war, some until 1948. Those with good conduct records were used to clear sites for rebuilding, or worked the land, for which services their farmer employers had to pay the government. There was some disquiet in the civilian ranks as until June 1945 the prisoners, on British Army rations, were better fed than British civilians.

An assessment of the home defences

Between 1940 and 1941, Britain had defended herself alone for a year, threatened by invasion and isolated, until Russia and the USA joined her in the struggle. Were the defences a success in themselves, or was Britain fortunate that the attention of the Wehrmacht was turned to the East?

On September 1940, at the time of the anticipated launching of Operation SEALION, Ironside's successor, Alan Brooke, confided in his diary that he felt that an invasion was a very real and probable threat and that, whilst the situation

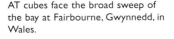

AT cubes face the broad sweep of the bay at Fairbourne, Gwynnedd, in Wales.

was not helpless, the land forces at his disposal did not give room for confidence. He anticipated a desperate struggle. It is clear that at the time of the anticipated invasion, because of the lack of AT guns, reliance had to be placed on weapons such as the Molotov Cocktail and the belief that 'tanks can be destroyed by men who have bravery, resource, and determination' (Local Defence Volunteer Instruction No 8, September 1940). This determination included, according to the Instruction, the suicidal action of pushing a pole with gun cotton explosive on the end from a street door into the tracks of a passing German tank.

However, the enemy's approach to London would not have been through ideal tank country. It would have been via narrow lanes, through closely packed towns, across the wooded Weald

A fate that has befallen many pillboxes: a collapsing 'Stent' prefabricated pillbox at Eckington Bridge, Worcestershire. The spaces between the panels were filled with a weak concrete mix. The foundations of the pillbox are being undermined by the River Avon, which in 1940 was one of the Midland stop-lines. (MW)

and through the few crossing points of the North Downs escarpment. Obstacles such as AT ditches, scarped riverbanks, canals, minefields, and bridge demolitions would delay the progress of German tanks. The German PzKpfw II and III tanks had relatively low climbing abilities of between two and three feet. But German assault pioneers had been adept at getting heavy equipment across the canals and the large, slow-flowing rivers of northern France in 1940. They had used pontoons, fast assault craft, inflatable boats (vulnerable to small-arms fire), and had provided temporary bridging and ramps to cross AT obstacles. The assault engineers also possessed flamethrowers and pole charges for the reduction of hardened defences such as pillboxes. If Britain had been lavishly equipped with AT guns, the invaders would surely have faced severe problems: the difficulties encountered by Allied tanks in the Bocage country of Normandy in 1944 comes readily to mind. But this was not the case in summer 1940 where troops and the Home Guard would have been sent out tank hunting fuelled only by the petrol in their Molotovs and their own bravery.

The British defensive commanders put much faith in the pillbox: yet, as we have already noted, it would not fare well against high-explosive projectiles and deadly accurate fire. The Germans had experience of dealing with the Maginot Line fortifications and other sites such as Eben Emael. Whilst it is possible that many of the AT islands could have been by-passed by the enemy the crowded nature of much of the British countryside, together with its dense road and rail system, would have forced the Germans through towns, villages and cities. The experiences at Stalingrad and Caen, where a determined defence could be achieved even in heavily bombed areas, show that even the effectiveness of armour is limited in urban fighting. The blockage of streets or roads by debris, the ease of creating strongholds in the ruins, and the danger posed by infantry AT weapons concealed in buildings would certainly disrupt the passage of tanks. The defences and the defenders of airfields, HAA batteries (whose 3.7in. guns could also be used in an AT role), radar and other military sites would have added their weight to the defence of their particular localities as and when required.

Had the Germans launched the invasion of Russia in May 1941 and not June, Britain might have faced imminent invasion once again in the autumn of that year. Assuming Germany's losses in the Soviet Union were not grave following an earlier start to BARBAROSSA, she would be in a strong position to

A surviving 'shell-proof' pillbox of the Bristol defences at Avening, Gloucestershire, which would have faced an AT ditch. This pillbox uses concrete panels as permanent shuttering and is based on the War Office Fortifications and Works design FW3/24 of 1940.

consider SEALION once more. Her eastern borders would have been secured, her army buoyant with victory, and she would be rich with the spoils of war, chiefly oil from Baku, grain from the Ukraine, and armament production facilities taken over in the earlier occupations such as the giant Skoda works in the former Czechoslovakia. She would have an unlimited supply of forced labour too. Weapons that were not available in 1940, such as the enormous tank-carrying Messerschmitt Me 321 glider, would be brought into play. Britain, on the other hand, had yet to win in battle against German forces. The Battle of the Atlantic was going badly in late-1941, with more shipping being lost than could be replaced. Her army was still re-equipping and training.

In reality though, by autumn 1941 Britain had recovered from the shock of Dunkirk and was in a stronger position than previously. Additionally, although Russia continued to fight, the fear always remained that she might sue for peace with Germany. Britain had to show Russia between 1941 and 1943 that she was not fighting alone and unaided on the continent, and so she sent Russia tanks, aircraft and other equipment she could ill afford to spare and at great cost in the lives of her sailors. Stalin pressed strenuously for a second front in Europe, but Britain could do little until the Allied forces were in a position to launch OVERLORD in June 1944. The invasion of Italy had stalled after its launch in 1943 and until D-Day Britain could only point to the bombing offensive by the RAF and USAAF against Germany to show that she was destroying or tying down German resources and manpower.

Russia's continuation of her epic struggle against the German invaders ensured that there was never any question of German forces re-engaging SEALION: resources would simply not allow for this. The arrival from 1942 onwards of American forces in Britain also precluded an invasion. By 1943, with the possible exception of occasional sabotage raids launched against her, Britain could largely discount the threat of SEALION: The successful invasion of France in 1944 left no doubt that the risk of invasion was now firmly over.

A final thought should be given to the threat posed to Britain by the V weapons. Had Germany been able to develop its programme sooner and launched a constant V2 and V3 barrage against Britain when still isolated and vulnerable, or when the Allies were still preparing for the D-Day landings, the effects might have been catastrophic.

The home defences today

The Defence of Britain project

The 50th anniversary of the end of the war in Europe reawakened an interest in home defence remains in Britain. A project called the Defence of Britain was launched in 1995, initiated by the Fortress Study Group. It brought together volunteers, local authorities and national heritage bodies and was administered by the Council for British Archaeology. Its aim was to create a database not only of surviving structures but also of those that had been destroyed. The best remaining examples would be the subject of statutory protection by UK national heritage bodies, such as English Heritage.

At the launch of the project it was confidently predicted that the location of all or most of the World War II defensive sites could be obtained by reference to the records held in the Public Record Office (now the National Archives): fieldwork could then be directed to these sites. In a parallel operation under English Heritage's Monuments Protection Programme, the PRO was searched for details of sites built during the war. This operation gave the locations for many categories of site, for example HAA batteries, but the location of small defensive sites such as pillboxes was more problematic as there was no consistent remaining record. The search for such sites was therefore a matter of fieldwork and the following of known stop-lines. This is not to say that

The Defence of Britain project, which began in 1995, involved the recording of surviving and destroyed sites. Here volunteers and archaeologists are recording a Bofors LAA gun site at Redditch, Worcestershire. This site would soon disappear with the construction of a new road. The author is on the left of this picture, in the light top.

records were entirely lacking. A search through Army War Diaries and the small number of surviving Home Guard records yielded some detailed defence schemes. Airfield plans held by the RAF Museum at Hendon often showed the location of defensive sites, and in aerial photographs taken in a survey just after the war and now held by the National Monuments Record the lines of AT ditches and pillboxes could often be seen. Another source of information was provided by the oblique and annotated aerial photographs taken by the Luftwaffe of British beach defences: these now reside in the USA.

The project was able to locate 6,000 of the 20,000-plus pillboxes built during the war. The highest rate of survival tends to be in country areas. Although much was cleared away after World War II, those sites not causing an obstruction were left intact. Sometimes these have been put to good use, for example as garden sheds, bat roosts, fishermen's huts, or even (following conversion) into public toilets. This is not to say that they will remain intact forever. Many have subsided into the rivers or down onto the beaches they were built to defend.

Surviving sites

With regard to other anti-invasion defence devices, the sockets for steel rails can still be found on some canal bridges. In the post-war period, millions of AT cylinders (used as buffers in front of the steel-rail AT obstacles) were gathered up from their original positions and reinvented as beach erosion defences, riverbank revetments, car park bollards, and even as the foundations for animal climbing structures found in certain zoos. Others were used as weights to keep tractor noses down in difficult ground. The shiny stainless steel pin on a concrete pedestal sticking up out of the ground above a filled-in Spigot Mortar pit is still a common find. Following the line of a stop-line will reveal many of the surviving defences: the pillboxes along the Kennet and Avon Canal in Berkshire, part of the GHQ Line, are fine surviving examples.

Along the coast, many batteries remain in a good condition, for example those at South Sutor in Scotland, Soldier's Rock at Milford Haven in Wales, Freiston in Lincolnshire, and the 6in. battery contained within the defences of Pendennis Castle in Cornwall.

A proportion of the country's wartime HAA batteries were carefully maintained after the war, due to the perceived threat from the Soviet Union. There are several good examples of surviving batteries, for example that at Bywaters Farm in Essex. Other hardened AA defences remain too, such as the bunkers provided for the generators and crews of bombing decoy sites. Many pre-war and wartime aircraft hangars, of immense strength, are still in use by the RAF, whilst others are in private hands and are used for the storage of all manner of goods. The pre-war and wartime hangars at the Imperial War Museum at Duxford near Cambridge are worth a visit.

Some of the buildings that served as administrative and technical centres during the war have also survived. Two of the most popular sites open to visitors are the Cabinet War Rooms in London and Western Approaches in Liverpool. The many thousands of common air-raid shelters have largely succumbed to the passing of time. The many large country houses requisitioned in the war have returned to more peaceful uses. Who could now believe that the grounds of Kedleston Hall in Derbyshire, now in National Trust hands, once housed hundreds of women of the Army Auxiliary Territorial Service employed on 'Y' intercept work? Beaumanor Park in Leicestershire, used as the War Office 'Y' Group headquarters, is now a county educational establishment, although several of the wartime-camouflaged outbuildings remain. The thousands of mass-produced, prefabricated, corrugated steel Romney and Nissen huts, together with equal numbers of timber and curved asbestos huts, provided useful emergency housing after the war: many were dismantled to be sold to farmers and others as handy store and cattle buildings.

Chronology

1937	Air Raid Precautions Act passed.
1 September 1939	Germany invades Poland: the evacuation of children from British cities begins.
3 September 1939	Britain declares war on Germany: conscription of men for the armed forces.
4 September 1939	Movement of British Expeditionary Force to France.
14 October 1939	Aerial attacks on Britain begin with the sinking of HMS *Royal Oak*.
February 1940	Interim defence plan issued for the port of Dover.
9 April 1940	Germany invades Norway and Denmark.
10 May 1940	Churchill becomes Prime Minister and Minister of Defence. Germany invades Belgium and Holland. French Army and BEF move into Belgium.
14 May 1940	Formation of LDV/Home Guard.
15 June 1940	Gen. Ironside issues national defence plan. Pillbox designs are issued. Work begins on the GHQ line.
22 June 1940	France surrenders.
28 June 1940	German forces occupy the Channel Islands: preparations for invasion are to be ready by mid-August 1940.
10 July 1940	Battle of Britain begins.
16 July 1940	Hitler issues Directive 16 to initiate Operation SEALION.
20 July 1940	Gen. Sir Alan Brooke becomes C-in-C, Home Forces. A move away from the static warfare concept of stop-lines begins.
7 September 1940	Luftwaffe switches emphasis to the night-bombing of London: the Blitz begins.
March 1941	The concept of AT islands starts to supersede the stop-line philosophy.
Spring 1941	The Home Guard begins to receive its 'sub-artillery' and mobile 6pdr improvised AT guns.
22 June 1941	BARBAROSSA commences: the threat of an invasion of Britain recedes for the time being.
7 December 1941	The United States enters the war. The threat of invasion recedes further.
23 February 1942	All work on building pillboxes ends: the pillbox becomes obsolete.
6 June 1944	OVERLORD, the invasion of Europe, begins. The clearance of anti-invasion defences is started.
13 June 1944	The first V1 weapon lands on London.
27 March 1945	The last V2 weapon lands.
8 May 1945	The war in Europe ends.

At the end of the war production in aircraft factories moved to the construction of comfortable pre-fabricated houses. This 'pre-fab' is at the Imperial War Museum at Duxford, Cambridgeshire.

Bibliography

Alanbrooke, Field Marshal Lord *War Diaries 1939–1945* (London, 2001)

Alexander, Colin *Ironside's Line* (West Sussex, 1998)

Bauer, Lt. Col. E. *The History of World War II* (London, 1979)

Bond, Brian *Britain, France and Belgium 1939–1940* (London, 1990)

Brettingham, Laurie *Royal Air Force Beam Benders: No. 80 (Signals) Wing 1941–45* (Leicester, 1997)

Calder, Angus *The People's War* (London, 1992)

Churchill, Winston *The Second World War*, Vol II (London, 1949)

Clarke, N.J. *Adolf Hitler's Home Counties Holiday Snaps: Luftwaffe target reconnaissance 1939–1942* (Lyme Regis, 1996)

Collier, Basil *The Defence of the United Kingdom* (London, 1957)

Dobinson, Colin *Twentieth Century Fortifications in England*, 10 vols (York, 1998: unpublished reports)

Dobinson, Colin *Fields of Deception* (London, 2000)

Dobinson, Colin *AA Command* (London, 2001)

Fleming, Peter *Invasion 1940* (London, 1957)

Foot, M.R.D. *SOE 1940–46* (London, 1984)

GHQ Home Forces, *Home Guard Instruction No. 51: Battlecraft and Battle Drill for the Home Guard, Part IV Organisation of Home Guard Defence*

GHQ Home Forces, *Home Guard Instruction No. 68: The 3in. OSB Gun (Smith Gun)*

Gilman, Peter and Leni *'Collar the Lot!' – How Britain interned and expelled its wartime refugees* (London, 1980)

Grant, Ian and Maddren, Nicholas *The Countryside at War* (London, 1975)

Graves, Charles *Home Guard of Britain* (London, 1943)

Hayward, James *Shingle Street: Flame, chemical and psychological warfare in 1940* (Colchester, 1994)

Her Majesty's Stationery Office *Roof over Britain* (London, date unknown)

Horne, Alistair *To Lose a Battle: France 1940* (London, 1969)

Inglis, Ruth *The Children's War: Evacuation 1939–1945* (London, 1990)

Jones, R.V. *Most Secret War* (London, 1978)

Kieser, Egbert *Hitler on the Doorstep: Operation Sealion, the German plan to invade Britain 1940* (London, 1997)

Lampe, David *The Last Ditch* (London, 1968)

Longmate, Norman *Air Raid: the bombing of Coventry 1940* (London, 1976)

Longmate, Norman *Doodlebug* (London, 1981)

Longmate, Norman *How we lived then* (London, 1971)

Longmate, Norman *If Britain had fallen* (London, 1972)

Longmate, Norman *Island Fortress: the defence of Great Britain 1603–1945* (London, 1993)

Longmate, Norman *The Real Dad's Army* (London, 1974)

Lowry, Bernard and Wilks, Mick *The Mercian Maquis: the secret resistance organisation in Herefordshire and Worcestershire in WW2* (Leominster, 2002)

Lowry, Bernard (ed.) *Twentieth Century Defences in Britain: an introductory handbook* (York, 1995)

Mackenzie, S.P. *The Home Guard* (Oxford 1995)

Macleod, Col. R. *The Ironside Diaries 1937–1940* (London, 1962)

McCamley, N.J. *Secret Underground Cities* (Barnsley, 1998)

National Archives, Kew: relevant files in the WO166/ and WO199/ series

Pile, Gen. Sir Frederick *Ack-Ack* (London, 1949)

Ramsey, Winston *The Blitz: then and now.* 3 vols (London, 1987)

Ramsey, Winston *The War in the Channel Islands: then and now* (London, 1981)

Redfern, Neil *Twentieth Century Fortifications in the UK*, 5 vols (York, 1998, unpublished reports)

Reynolds, David *Rich Relations: The American Occupation of Britain 1942–1945* (London, 1995)

Schellenberg, Walter *Invasion 1940: the Nazi invasion plan for Britain* (London, 2000)

Slater, Hugh *Home Guard for Victory* (London, 1941)

Smith, David J. *British Military Airfields 1939–45* (Wellingborough, 1989)

Spender, Stephen *Citizens in War and After* (London, 1945)

The War Office *Field Engineering (All Arms) Pamphlet No. 30: Part III, Obstacles* (1940)

The War Office *Field Engineering (All Arms) Pamphlet No. 30: Part III, Obstacles* (1943)

The War Office *Home Guard Instruction No. 40: The Northover Projector* (1941)

The War Office *Small Arms Training Vol. I, Pamphlet 23: the 29mm Spigot Mortar* (1942)

Twinch, Carol *Women on the Land: their story during two World Wars* (Cambridge, 1990)

Tyner, Nicola *They fought in the fields – The Women's Land Army: the story of a forgotten victory* (London, 1996)

West, Nigel *GCHQ: the secret wireless war 1900–86* (London, 1987)

Wills, Henry *Pillboxes: a study of UK defences 1940* (London, 1985)

Wintringham, Tom *New Ways of War* (London, 1940)

Wintringham, Tom *Peoples' War* (London, 1942)

Wood, Derek *Attack Warning Red: the Royal Observer Corps and the defence of Britain 1925–1992* (London, 1976)

Glossary and abbreviations

AA   Anti-aircraft.
AT   Anti-tank.
ADGB   Air Defence of Great Britain organisation.
AP   Anti-personnel.
ARP   Air Raid Precautions.
ATS   Auxiliary Territorial Service.
A4   Abbreviation of Aggregat 4, an alternative name for the V2.
BEF   British Expeditionary Force.
Blitzkrieg   Literally 'lightning war'.
CASL   Coast Artillery Searchlight.
CH   The Chain Home radar system. Later developed into the Chain Home Low (CHL) and Chain Home Extra Low (CHEL) systems.
Fallschirmjäger   German airborne troops (part of the Luftwaffe).
Fleet Air Arm   Aviation element of the Royal Navy.
Flak   Fliegerabwehrkanone (AA gun operated by the Luftwaffe).
GCHQ   Government Communications Headquarters.
Gebirgsjäger   German mountain troops.
GHQ   General Headquarters.
GHQ Line   The main defensive stop-line built in response to the expected German invasion in 1940, consisting of a system of static defences such as pillboxes, AT obstacles, minefields and defended positions.
Heer   The German Army (part of the Wehrmacht).
LAA   Light anti-aircraft artillery.
HAA   Heavy anti-aircraft artillery.
Knickebein   ('Dog's-leg' beam): an early-type German navigation and bombing aid.
Kriegsmarine   The German Navy (part of the Wehrmacht).
LDV   Local Defence Volunteers.
Luftwaffe   The German Air Force (part of the Wehrmacht).
Northover Projector   A short-range, grenade-firing weapon consisting of a smoothbore barrel with a hinged breech, and standing on a four-legged base; for AT or AP use.
OKM   Oberkommando der Marine, the German Navy High Command.

OKW   Oberkommando der Wehrmacht, the German Armed Forces High Command.
OSB   Ordnance Smooth Bore.
Phantom   A codename for the GHQ Liaison Regiment.
PIAT   Projector, Infantry (AT Weapon).
PRU   Photographic Reconnaisance Unit.
QF (gun)   Quick-firing.
QF (decoy)   A fire decoy used to divert German bombers to false targets.
QL   Lighting effect decoys, used to divert enemy bombers.
RA   The Royal Artillery.
RAF   The Royal Air Force.
Regia Aeronautica   The Italian Air Force.
ROC   The Royal Observer Corps.
SAS   The Special Air Service.
SD   Sicherheitsdienst, the security and counter intelligence service of the SS.
SIP   Self-Igniting Phosphorous (grenade).
SOE   Special Operations Executive.
Staffel   A Luftwaffe squadron.
SS   Schutzstaffel, the Nazi Party's protection organisation.
Stuka   Common abbreviation for Sturzkampfflugzeug, literally a 'diving warplane'.
USAAF   US Army Air Force.
V1/V2/V3   Vergeltungswaffe (literally 'vengeance weapon') 1/2/3.
Waffen-SS   Armed branch of the Schutzstaffel.
Wehrmacht   Literally 'defence force'; the German armed forces of World War II, comprising the Heer, Luftwaffe and Kriegsmarine.
WAAF   Women's Auxiliary Air Force.
'Y' Service   Codename for wireless intercept service.
WLA   Women's Land Army.
WVS   Women's Voluntary Service.
'X'-Apparatus   (X-Geräte): A mid-version German beamed navigation and bombing aid.
'Y'-Apparatus   (Y-Geräte): A later-version, sophisticated German beamed navigation and bombing aid.
'Z' rocket   AA weapon officially known as the 'UP' or 'unrotated projectile'.

Index